THE USBORNE
COMPUTER
DICTIONARY

Anna Claybourne and Mark Wallace

Designed by Paul Greenleaf, Russell Punter and Michèle Busby

Illustrated by Andy Burton

Edited by Kamini Khanduri and Lisa Miles

Technical consultant: Richard Payne

Photography by Howard Allman

Additional consultancy by Tom Barry, Nick Bell, Marc Carey, Liam Devany, Nigel Hooper and Fiona Sanderson

Cover design by Zöe Wray

Contents

Introduction

This book is a guide to **computer jargon** - the words and phrases used to describe computers and everything related to them. Computers have developed so quickly that hundreds of new jargon words are being used to describe things that never existed before. Some computer words, like mouse, bus and virus, are normal words that have new meanings in computer jargon. Others, such as cyberspace, modem and dongle, are completely new words. There are even jargon words for "computer jargon". It can be called **computerspeak**, **technospeak**, **cyberspeak**, or **technobabble**.

Many of the words in this dictionary have been chosen to be useful to people who use a personal computer or home computer. But lots of other subjects are covered too, such as how computers work, computer history, computer culture, and what might happen in the future.

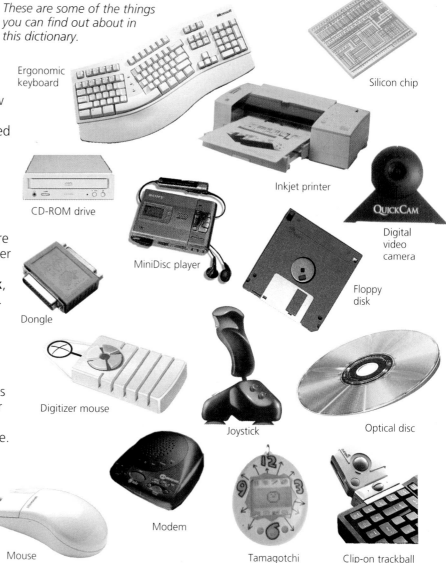

These are some of the things you can find out about in this dictionary.

Ergonomic keyboard

Silicon chip

Inkjet printer

CD-ROM drive

MiniDisc player

Digital video camera

Dongle

Floppy disk

Digitizer mouse

Joystick

Optical disc

Graphics tablet

Modem

Mouse

Tamagotchi

Clip-on trackball

 Using this dictionary

Instead of being arranged with all the words in alphabetical order, this dictionary is arranged by subject. For example, you can find out about computer graphics on pages 36-39, or about printers on pages 10-11.

Wherever a computer word or phrase is defined or explained, the word is printed in bold type, like this: **mouse**. If a word is explained in more detail on another page, it is printed in italic type, with an asterisk, like this: *mouse**. At the bottom of the page you will find a page number showing where to find the explanation.

To find an explanation of a particular word, first look it up in the index. The main explanation of the word is on the page shown in the index in bold type, like this: **37**. Other page numbers show other pages the word appears on.

The glossaries at the end of the book contain extra words, computer slang, and a quick guide to computer acronyms (letters that stand for words) such as RAM, ROM and VDU.

Essential computer words

A **computer** is any machine that takes in and stores **data** (information), does calculations, and gives out the results. Modern computers run on electricity and are very fast and accurate. They can work on, or **process**, all sorts of data, such as numbers, words, pictures and sounds. Many of the things computers can do are explained in this dictionary.

Input is the information fed into a computer.

Processing is the work done by a computer.

Output is the data given out by a computer.

Hardware is the machinery that makes up a computer - the solid parts, like the *keyboard**, *monitor** and *processing unit**. **Software** is the name for the instructions a computer is given so that it can do pieces of work, known as **jobs** or **tasks**. A set of instructions is called a *program**.

A **computer system** is a set of hardware and software. A **function** is something a computer can do. A computer's **functionality** is the range of things it can do. A computer that is switched on and working is said to be **up and running**, **live**, **on line** or **busy**.

A person who uses a computer system is called the **user**, or **end user**. A system that is easy to use is described as **user-friendly**. A system that is hard to use is **user-unfriendly**.

Types and uses

All computers work in basically the same way, but there are lots of different types. Most of the information in this book is about **home computers**. These are small computers that can be used by one person.

A **personal computer** or **PC** is the most common kind of home computer. PCs are based on a brand of computer called the *IBM PC**, which was first made in 1981.

A *Mac** (short for Apple Macintosh) is a brand of computer which is similar to a PC, but is built differently inside. The way a computer is designed and built is called its **architecture**.

If you have a computer at home or at school, it is probably a PC or a Mac. Full-sized home computers, like the one in the big picture opposite, are called **desktop PCs**. There are also smaller PCs such as *notebooks**.

Larger computers such as *mainframes** are not home computers. They can work much faster than PCs and process more data at once. They are usually used by business people and scientists.

Many everyday machines such as washing machines and videos are **computerized** - they contain computers to help them work faster. Computers are also increasingly being used to control and organize many processes, such as storing information, communicating, and banking. This growth in the use of computers is sometimes called **digitization**. The word **digital** is used to describe a system that uses digits, or numbers, and is often used in relation to computers.

Storing data

While a computer is switched on, data can be stored in its *memory**. When it is switched off, most of this data is lost. To keep data safe, you have to *save** it, on a *storage device** such as the *hard disk** or a *floppy disk**. Storage devices are a vital part of any computer system.

Floppy disk

Window

Disk guard

Plastic case   Disk hub

This picture shows a personal computer with a monitor, keyboard, mouse and printer.

A keyboard* is used to type data into the computer. It has several different kinds of keys.

Key

Keyboard

*The space a computer takes up on a table top is called its **footprint**.*

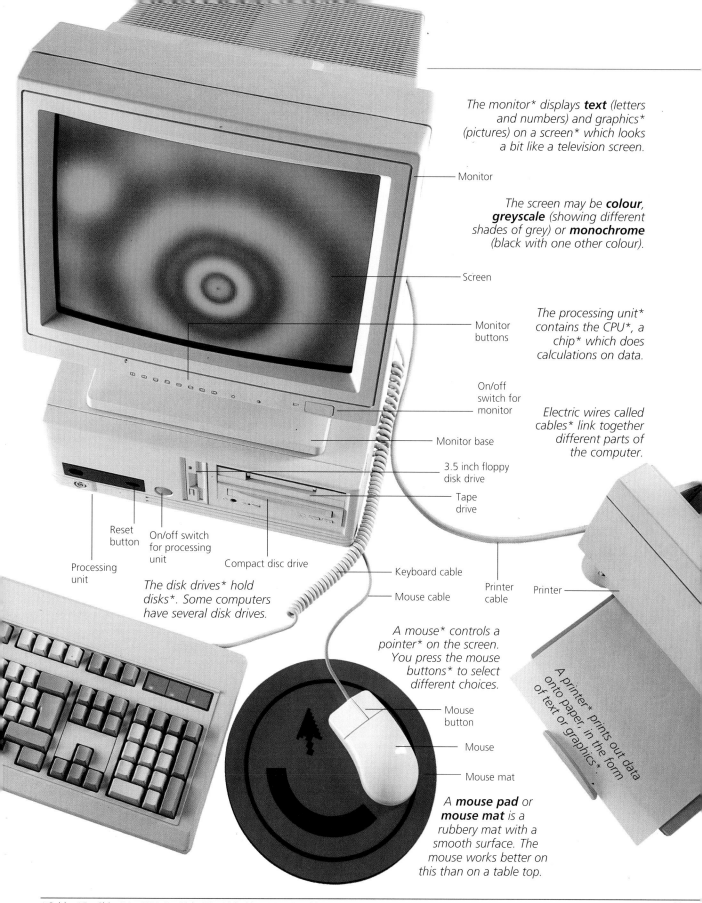

The monitor* displays **text** (letters and numbers) and graphics* (pictures) on a screen* which looks a bit like a television screen.

Monitor

The screen may be **colour**, **greyscale** (showing different shades of grey) or **monochrome** (black with one other colour).

Screen

The processing unit* contains the CPU*, a chip* which does calculations on data.

Monitor buttons

On/off switch for monitor

Electric wires called cables* link together different parts of the computer.

Monitor base

3.5 inch floppy disk drive

Tape drive

Reset button

On/off switch for processing unit

Compact disc drive

Processing unit

The disk drives* hold disks*. Some computers have several disk drives.

Keyboard cable

Mouse cable

Printer cable

Printer

A mouse* controls a pointer* on the screen. You press the mouse buttons* to select different choices.

Mouse button

Mouse

Mouse mat

A printer* prints out data onto paper, in the form of text or graphics*.

A **mouse pad** or **mouse mat** is a rubbery mat with a smooth surface. The mouse works better on this than on a table top.

---

*Cable, 17; Chip, 21; CPU, 9; Disk, 23; Disk drive, 23; Graphics, 36; Monitor, 7; Mouse, 7; Mouse button, 7; Pointer, 7; Printer, 10; Processing unit, 8; Screen, 7

Input and output devices

A computer does all its processing in numbers. For people to communicate, or **interact**, with a computer, these numbers have to be translated into a language they can understand. **Input devices**, such as the keyboard, translate data from the user and carry it, or **input** it, into the computer. **Output devices**, such as the monitor, translate the results and send, or **output**, them back to the user. The keyboard, mouse and monitor are the basic input and output devices on most *PCs**, but there are many other kinds.

Input devices can carry all kinds of data into computers, such as *text**, *sound** and pictures. For example, a **barcode reader**, or **barcode scanner**, is used in shops to read **barcodes** (price labels made up of black and white stripes) and send the price back to a computer in the till.

Barcode reader

Output devices can give you all sorts of output, such as *graphics**, *printouts** and public messages. For example, **computerized public displays** and **dot matrix indicators** show moving messages in shops or at stations and airports. The messages are *programmed** into a computer which is linked to the display.

Computerized public display

NEXT TRAIN.....3 MINS

The keyboard

The **keyboard** usually has **alphanumeric** (letter and number) **keys** on it, arranged in the same pattern as on a typewriter (called the **QWERTY** pattern). There are also extra keys, called dedicated keys (see below) and function keys (see right). There are different kinds of keyboards on many *computerized** machines, such as the *keypad** on a TV remote control, and the *control panel** on a microwave oven. You may also see **touch-sensitive keyboards** with panels on a flat surface instead of raised keys.

- **Function keys** These can be programmed to do special jobs.
- **Numeric keypad** A pad with numbers arranged like those on a calculator, to make it easy to use.
- **Cursor control keys** Keys that move a cursor (see facing page).
- **Space bar** Puts a space on the screen between **characters** (letters, numbers and symbols).
- **PAGE UP** and **PAGE DOWN keys** These let you **scroll**, or move your *document**, up and down on the screen to look at different parts of it.
- **Keyboard feet** Little pegs under the keyboard. They tilt the keyboard towards you so it is more comfortable to use.

A typical computer keyboard

Keyboard feet underneath — Alphanumeric keys — Function keys — PAGE UP and PAGE DOWN keys — Keyboard cable

CAPS LOCK key — SHIFT key — Space bar — RETURN or ENTER key — Cursor control keys — Numeric keypad

Dedicated keys

Dedicated keys have a word or symbol on them. They give the computer a particular instruction.

*The **RETURN** or **ENTER** key (sometimes an arrow symbol) is pressed at the end of an instruction to tell the computer to carry it out.*

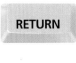
RETURN

ENTER

*Keys such as **SHIFT** and **CONTROL** change the function of other keys. Some computers also have a **Windows** or **Apple key**.*

*Toggle keys, such as **CAPS LOCK** and **INSERT**, are pressed once to start working, and again to go back to normal.*

SHIFT

CONTROL

CAPS LOCK

INSERT

Computerized, 4; Control panel, 15; Document, 25; Graphics, 36; Keypad, 27; PC, 4, 12; Printout, 10; Programming, 44; Sound, 40; Text, 5; Windows, 26

The mouse

A **mouse** (plural: **mouses** or **mice**) moves a **pointer** on the screen. You use a mouse by moving it across a *mouse pad**. You **select** an instruction from the screen by **clicking** (pressing and releasing) or **double clicking** (pressing twice) on a **mouse button**. **Clicking and dragging** means holding down a button as you move the mouse. Some mouses include a **scrolling wheel**, which is used to scroll (see facing page) down the page.

An **ergonomic mouse** is curved to fit your hand. Most mouses are linked to the computer by a *cable** or **tail**. Mouses without tails are called **cordless** or **tail-less mouses**.

Inside a right-handed ergonomic mouse

Plastic casing

Light detector

Mouse button

Roller

Mouse ball

LED

Light patterns

Slot

Encoder

These send information back to the computer in the form of infra-red light signals.

When you move a mouse, a rubber **mouse ball** inside rolls across the pad. The ball turns two **rollers**, which turn wheels called **encoders**. Tiny lights called **LEDs** (**Light-Emitting Diodes**) shine light through slots in the encoders to make light

patterns. These are sensed by **light detectors** and turned into information about how the mouse has moved.

A **touchpad** or **trackpad** is a touch-sensitive pad. You can use it by touching it with a finger, or by pressing a button at the side to move a pointer. Touchpads are most commonly found on *notebooks**.

The monitor

The **monitor** or **VDU** (**Visual Display Unit**) shows you data on a **screen** and displays different options. There are two main kinds of monitor. *Liquid Crystal Display** (LCD) monitors are often used with notebooks. **CRT** (**Cathode Ray Tube**) **monitors** are large and look like televisions. They usually have **graphics adaptors** - devices which give a monitor high-quality *graphics**. Two common types of graphics adaptor are: **VGA** (**Video Graphics Array**) or **SVGA** (**Super Video Graphics Array**).

The picture on a monitor's screen is called an **image**. A monitor's **resolution** means the sharpness of its image. A **high resolution** image is made up of small dots and is very clear and sharp. A **low resolution** image is made up of larger dots, and does not show such clear and realistic pictures.

• The resolution depends on the number of dots, or **pixels** (short for **picture elements**) that make up the screen. A modern SVGA monitor has over a million pixels.
• **Glare** means the screen reflects light and damages your eyes. Some screens have an **anti-glare filter** to reduce glare.
• The monitor gives out a small amount of harmful **radiation**. **Low-radiation** or **low-rad**

monitors give out less radiation.
• A **cursor** shows where the next character (see facing page) you type will appear.
• A **degauss button** gets rid of static electricity, which stops the screen from working properly.
• **Brightness** and **contrast buttons** let you alter the image.
• **Size controls** and **centre controls** move and stretch the image on the screen.

This picture shows a CRT monitor and some of the things you might see on it.

Pixel

Degauss button

Size and centre controls

Base

Screen

Image

On/off switch

Contrast button

Brightness button

Inside the processing unit

The **processing unit** is the main part of a computer, where data is stored and processed. It is also called the **systems unit**, and sometimes just the **computer** or even the **hard disk** (although the *hard disk** is just one part of it). It is made up of *chips** and several other parts inside a strong *case**.

The chips and other devices are arranged on plastic boards called **PCBs (Printed Circuit Boards)**. The main PCB is called the **motherboard** or **mainboard**, and smaller PCBs joined onto it are called **daughterboards** or **cards**. Printed pathways, called **tracks**, make up **electrical circuits**, which carry data around the computer.

Tracks are usually arranged in groups called *buses**. Data travels along the buses from one chip to another. Buses contain slots called **expansion slots**. You can fit extra PCBs called **expansion cards** into these to improve your *PC's** performance - for example, to give it better *sound** or *graphics**.

 ## On the front

There are several buttons on the front of the processing unit. The **on/off switch** starts your computer working (known as **booting up**). You can boot up again (**reboot**), without switching off completely, by pressing the **reset button**. Lights called **LED indicators** show that the computer is on, and a **loud-speaker** makes sounds.

The *hard disk drive** fits into spare space inside the *case**. *Floppy disk drives** and *CD-ROM drives** fit into **drive bays** in the front of the processing unit.

 ## Ports

A **port**, or **I/O port** (short for **Input/Output port**) is a socket in the back of the processing unit that allows you to connect *input and output devices** to it. On a PC there are usually two kinds of port: *parallel ports** and *serial ports**. Some ports are for specific uses, such as the **mouse port** and the **keyboard port**. Some computers have a **SCSI (Small Computer System Interface) port**, which works more quickly than a parallel or

This picture shows some of the parts inside the processing unit more clearly.

serial port. Another type of port is the **USB (Universal Serial Bus) port**, which allows more devices to be added to a computer more easily.

Interfaces

An **interface** is an electrical circuit which controls and adapts the signals passing between the processing unit and another piece of *hardware**. There are several types of interface.

RAM chips

BIOS (Basic Input/Output System)

ROM chips

Expansion card

Clock

Heatsink

Loudspeaker

BIOS

Main PCB or motherboard

CPU or Central Processing Unit

On/off switch

ROM and RAM

A computer has two main kinds of *memory**. *ROM** stores the instructions that tell the computer how to start working. The **BIOS (Basic Input/Output System)** is usually part of ROM and contains instructions for running the *input and output devices**. *RAM** stores data while the computer is working on it, but loses this data when you switch the computer off.

Power supply

Capacitor

Resistor

Drive bays

The CPU

The **Central Processing Unit** or **CPU** (also called the **processor** or **microprocessor**) is the "brain" of a computer. It is a large *chip** (or group of chips) that controls all the computer's calculations, or **operations**.

Diagram of the main parts of a CPU chip

Prefetch unit

Decode unit

Bus interface unit

Execution unit

Control unit

Protection test unit

Registers

ALU

Different CPUs have different kinds of structure, or *architecture**, but they all work in a similar way. This list explains what the main parts of a CPU do.
- **Bus interface unit** fetches instructions from RAM and passes them to the decode unit.
- **Prefetch unit** keeps the instructions in a queue, ready to pass on to the decode unit.
- **Decode unit** translates each instruction so that it is ready to be processed.
- **Execution unit** is the part that does the actual processing. It has four main sections:
- **Control unit** sends instructions to other parts of the execution unit, for example to collect data, do calculations and send the results to RAM.
- **Protection test unit** checks for **errors** (mistakes).
- **Registers** hold pieces of data that are being calculated.
- **Arithmetic Logic Unit** (**ALU**) performs the calculations.

Power and speed

Computers work at various speeds, depending on the individual computer's clock speed and processing power.

The **clock** is a device that sends electrical signals called **pulses** around the computer. On each pulse, or **clock cycle**, the computer does one calculation (on some computers it can do several). A *PC** has a **clock speed** (or **clock rate**) such as 450 million **clock cycles per second** (450 **megahertz** or **Mhz**).

Processing power is the speed at which the CPU works. The speed depends on the kind of CPU a computer has. Most PCs have *Intel** CPUs, such as the *286**, *386**, *486**, *Pentium®**, **Pentium® Pro**, and *Pentium® II Processor*. *Macs** and many larger computers use different kinds of CPU.

Components

A processing unit contains many electronic parts, or **components**. These include the **power supply**, which converts electricity from the mains supply into the right voltage for the computer, and **resistors** and **capacitors** which control the flow of electricity around the circuits. A **heatsink** is a piece of metal attached to a chip. It stops the chip from getting too hot, which can stop it from working.

Capacitor   *Heatsink*

Resistor

Printers

Printers are *output devices**
that print out data, usually
onto paper. A piece of printed
*output** is called a **printout** or
hard copy. (**Soft copy** is data
held in an electronic form.)

There are several kinds of
printers with different ways of
working. Some can only print
*text**; others can print *graphics**
too. **Black and white printers**
are more common, while **colour
printers** are more expensive and
often slower. Printers work at
various speeds. **Character
printers** (or **serial printers**)
print one *character** at a time.
Line printers print one line at a
time and **page printers** print a
page at a time.

Printers are either impact or
non-impact. **Impact printers**
print by hitting an inked **printer
ribbon** against the paper. **Non-
impact printers** squirt or press
ink onto the paper. Most printers
use **ink cartridges** or **toner
cartridges** which can be
replaced when they run out.
Toner is powdered ink.

Printed images are usually
made up of thousands of tiny
dots. The smaller the dots, the
sharper and clearer the printout.
The sharpness of the printout is
called the **print resolution**.

Sending files

When you want to print a *file**
you have to **send** it to a printer.
Most computers are linked to a
printer by a **printer cable**. Some
*dedicated word processors**
have a **built-in printer**.

A *program** in your computer,
called a **printer driver**, converts
your file into instructions for the
printer. A **print spooler** is a
program that organizes and
arranges any files that are
waiting to be printed.

 ## Types of printer

Most types of printer have the
same basic mechanism. A moving
print head prints from side to
side across the paper. The paper
is held by a large roller called a
platen and some smaller rollers
inside. A line feed (see facing
page) *function** moves the paper
up for each new line. Laser
printers (see facing page) work
in a different way.

Some different types of printer

Inkjet
printer

Laser
printer

Photo-quality
printer

• **Inkjet** or **bubblejet printers**
make up characters out of lots of
tiny ink droplets. They are
available to print in colour or
black and white. The print head
contains up to 50 **ink chambers**.
When each chamber is heated, a
drop of ink boils and bursts out
of a **nozzle** onto the paper.

Enlarged cross-section of an ink chamber — Ink — Paper — Nozzle — Chamber is heated here. — Ink squirts out of nozzle.

• **Colour printers** usually use a
process called **four-colour
printing**. Four colours - **black,
yellow, cyan** (a kind of
turquoise) and **magenta** (bright
pink) - are printed one at a time.
Combinations of these colours
make full-colour pictures. Colour
printers are usually inkjet
printers with four separate print
heads, one for each colour.
Some colour printers use **three-
colour printing** and have only
three colours (not black). They
make a kind of black, called
registration black, by
combining all three colours.

• **Photo-quality printers** use
either a similar method to
bubblejet printers, or a process
called **dye sublimation**. This
uses heat to transfer dye from a
ribbon onto a coating on the
paper. They print **continuous
tones** rather than dots onto
glossy **photographic paper**,
which can create a very high
quality image. They are often
used to print out photographs
taken by *digital cameras**.

• **Dot matrix printers** are
impact printers. They create
characters using a group, or
matrix, of tiny **printing pins** on
the print head. These press the
printer ribbon onto the paper.

• **Daisywheel printers** have a
large **daisywheel** on the print
head, with raised characters on
"**petals**" around the edge. The
wheel spins very quickly, while a
hammer pushes the petals
against the ribbon one at a time.

*Cable, 17; Character, 6; Dedicated word processor, 15; Digital Camera, 17; File, 25; Function, 4; Graphics, 36; Output, 4;
Output devices, 6; Program, 44; Text, 5

Laser printers

Laser printers are the fastest printers, and are available to print in black and white or colour. They use a **laser beam** (an intense beam of electrical power, or **charge**, on a roller called a **drum**. Toner (see facing page) sticks to the dots of charge, and the toner-covered drum is then pressed against the paper. The **fusing system** fixes the toner permanently.

Inside a laser printer

 # Printer words

- **cps** (**characters per second**) Describes printing speed. Fast dot matrix printers print at 150cps.
- **ppm** (**pages per minute**) A measure of fast speeds. Some laser printers print up to 20ppm.
- **dpi** (**dots per inch**) The number of dots that make up an inch of a printed image. The higher the dpi, the sharper the image.
- **Print server** or **printer server** A computer that holds *files** that are waiting to be printed, and stores them on its *hard disk** in a **print queue**. Print servers are used on *networks** where users share a printer (**print sharing**).
- **Image quality** The sharpness of a printout, measured in dpi. **NLQ** (**Near Letter Quality**) and **letter quality** are very sharp. Quicker **draft quality** is used when printouts don't have to look so good.
- **Memory buffer** A part of the printer's RAM that stores data that is waiting to be printed.
- **Consumables** Things that get used up, like paper, toner and printer ribbon (see facing page).
- **Bi-directional printing** This means the print head (see facing page) can print either from left to right or from right to left. **Logic-seeking print heads** save time by starting the next line at the side nearest to their last position.
- **Tractor** This feeds a supply of continuous stationery into the printer. Toothed wheels called **sprockets** hold the paper in the right place.

Labels: Fusing system · Mirror reflects laser beam onto drum. · Laser beam · Printed image on paper · Toner cartridge · The laser makes invisible dots of electrical charge here. · Drum · Paper · Paper tray

 # Printer memory

Like a computer, a printer has two kinds of *memory** - **printer ROM***, which holds instructions that make the printer work, and **printer RAM***, which stores data while the printer is switched on.

Printers use a **Page Description Language** (**PDL**) such as **PostScript**. A PDL lets you print detailed *graphics**. It gives the printer exact instructions describing how to draw the image on the page. Characters are described by sets of instructions called **outlines**.

 # Printer paper

Several kinds of paper are made specially for computer printers. **Continuous stationery** is a long strip of sheets joined together. It can be either **fanfold paper** (also called **accordion fold** or **concertina fold**) or **roll paper** (also called printer roll). Single pieces of paper are called **cut sheet paper**. Printers move, or **feed**, the paper upwards as they print. **Line feed** moves the paper line by line, and **form feed** moves it a page at a time. **Reverse feed** can move the paper backwards.

Certain types of paper are particularly suitable for inkjet printers (see facing page), which improve the quality of the images on the paper. These have a chemical coating, so that images can appear much more clearly. Photographic paper (see facing page) is commonly used for photo-quality printers (see facing page).

Fanfold paper

Roll paper

Continuous stationery · Tractor · Sprocket

Types of computer

There are thousands of types of computer, from tiny ones you can carry around, to large, complicated systems with hundreds of users.

The first computers were very big, because they contained lots of large parts. Small computers appeared when the *chip** was invented in the 1960s. A **personal computer**, or **PC**, is a small computer which has its own *processing unit**, *monitor** and *keyboard** and is usually used by one person.

Early PCs were called **microcomputers** or **micros**, because they were smaller than the computers that had existed before. One of the first was the *Altair**, made in 1971. In the 1980s, micros such as the **ZX81**, the **ZX Spectrum**, the **Vic 20**, the **Commodore 64** and the **BBC Computer** became very popular, and some people still use them. Most of these computers have their processing unit under the keyboard, and use a television as a monitor.

ZX Spectrum

People started using the name "PC" after the *IBM** **Personal Computer** was introduced in 1981. Soon other companies began making similar computers (known as **IBM clones**), and these started to be called PCs too. Now, **IBM-compatible** means a PC that works like an IBM PC, and can use the same pieces of *software**.

PCs come in various sizes and have different features. A list of these features is called a **specification** or **spec**.

Macs

A **Mac** (short for **Apple Macintosh**) is a kind of computer which is similar to IBM PCs and IBM clones (see left), but which has a different kind of *architecture**. A company called **Apple Computer** started making Macs in 1984. Macs are not IBM-compatible (see left), so they need different software. However, IBM and Apple have worked together to make the **Power PC** and the **Power Mac**, which can **emulate** (imitate) each other and so can use the same software.

Apple Macintosh computer

Cases

Modern PCs are made in various shapes. The box containing the processing unit is called the **case** or **chassis**. A flat case is called a **desktop case**.

Desktop case

A vertical case is called a **tower**. Towers can usually hold several *disk drives**. There are three main sizes of tower.

Full tower

Midi tower

Mini tower

Chip numbers

Many PCs are labelled "**Intel Inside®**", which means they use a *CPU** *chip** made by a company called **Intel**. A name such as **486** (short for **Intel 80486**) describes the type of Intel chip used. The higher the number, or **generation**, the more powerful the chip.

- **286** or **AT** The first well-known Intel chip used in PCs.
- **386SX** and **386DX** These chips have a bigger *bus** than the 286.
- **486SX** Has an internal *cache** (a kind of extra *memory**).
- **486DX** Has an internal cache and a *co-processor** (an extra processing chip).
- **486DX2** and **486DX4** Have faster *processing speeds** than the 486DX.
- **Pentium®** and **Pentium® II Processor** The current generation in the Intel family of chips. Has two caches and an extra-wide *64-bit bus**. **MMX®**is a component which improves the computer's *multimedia** performance.

Macs use **601**, **603**, and **604** chips, developed by Apple and IBM for Power PCs and Power Macs with a company called **Motorola**.

Upgrading

Upgrading means improving a PC's performance. A PC's **upgradability** means the extent to which it can be upgraded. A **fully upgradable** PC can have nearly all its parts replaced or added to. For example, a PC with **expandable RAM** can have more *RAM** chips added. A **user-removable CPU** can be taken out so a new one can be plugged in. **Zero Insertion Force** (**ZIF**) **sockets** are sockets inside the processing unit that are easy to plug chips into, so you can upgrade your own computer.

Shrinking PCs

Portable *PCs** can be closed up like a briefcase and carried around. The first portables (called **luggables** or **carry-and-park portables**) were quite heavy and had to be plugged in. Now, most portables are **notebooks**, also called **laptops** or **work-on-the-go portables**, which don't have to be plugged in. They have **NiCad** (**Nickel Cadmium**) or **NiMH** (**Nickel Metal Hydride**) rechargeable batteries, or **battery packs**.

Some notebooks can be plugged into a **docking station**, a base which turns the notebook into a *desktop PC**, with a full-sized *CRT monitor** and space for extra *expansion cards**. A **port replicator** is another type of base which connects a notebook to a larger system.

Instead of a *mouse**, notebooks often have a **trackball** (also called a **trackerball** or **thumbball**) built into the *keyboard**. You roll the ball with your hand to move a *pointer** on the screen. Sometimes notebooks have a **clip-on** or **snap-on** trackball instead,

Clip-on trackball

This is a notebook PC. It weighs about 3kg (6.5lb).

Lid
Keyboard
PC cards
Touchpad
TFT screen
Battery strength indicator
CD drive
Palm rest
Battery

which fits on the side of the keyboard, or a **pen mouse** or **ballpoint mouse**, a mouse shaped like a pen, with the ball in its tip, or a *touchpad**.
- The flat screen is usually an **LCD** (**Liquid Crystal Display**) **screen**, which works by shining light through a special liquid. **Dual scan LCD screens** replace, or **refresh**, the light on the screen twice as fast as normal or **standard passive LCD screens**.
- **TFT** (**Thin Film Transistor**) screens are a kind of flat screen. They are brighter than LCD screens and show more colours.
- A **detachable lid** allows the screen to be swapped for a newer, better one.
- **External** *ports**, or **outlets**, such as a keyboard port, link the notebook to full-size *input and output devices**.

- Some notebooks have **dual batteries**, so you can change, or **hot swap**, to a second battery when the first runs out. Meanwhile, a **RAM capacitor** keeps the notebook running.
- A **mains adaptor** lets a notebook use the mains electricity supply. An **autosensing power supply** can convert electricity from any mains socket.
- If you leave the notebook on, **auto suspend** makes it use less power, or **power down**. **Auto resume** makes it start working again when you press a key or move the mouse.
- A notebook can use a small internal or portable *modem** for connecting to a *network**. This means that people can work from home, and communicate easily with people in the office.

 ## Pocket PCs

Palmtops, also called **sub-notebooks** or **hand-held PCs**, are tiny PCs, even smaller than notebooks (see above). Some of them can run a version of *Microsoft®Windows®** called **Windows CE**. They can weigh less than 170g (6oz). You can carry one in your pocket, but you can use it to do many of the tasks you would do with a

portable PC.

Personal organizers or **electronic diaries** are tiny computers for storing notes, reminders and addresses. Some have **pen-based input** - you write straight onto the screen and the computer recognizes your writing with a **character recognition program**. You can also store data on tiny **memory cards** to keep it safe.

Palmtop

Personal organizer with pen-based input

More types of computer

Big computers

The first computers were much bigger than modern ones. In the mid-1800s, a scientist called **Charles Babbage** designed an early computer, called the *Analytical Engine**, but it was too large for him to build. The first electronic computer, *ENIAC**, built in 1945, was so big it took up an area as big as ten large cars.

Charles Babbage

Today, the biggest computers are **mainframes**, which are used to process very large amounts of data (called **number crunching**). They have a powerful *processing unit**, linked to many **terminals**. A terminal has a *monitor** and a *keyboard** for a user to work at. This is called **centralized**

computing. The processing unit is very sensitive and must be kept at the right temperature. It is often stored at a different place from the terminals, which are linked to it by a *network**. This is called **remote processing**.

Mainframes work by **timesharing**. This means that the users (called *end users** or **multiple users**) can all share the processing unit without interfering with each other's work. The computer appears to be doing lots of jobs at once. In fact, it quickly swaps between the different jobs. This is called **multitasking**. The mainframe in a large company is run by the **Data Processing (DP) department** or the **Information Technology (IT) department**.

Minicomputers are small mainframes. **Supercomputers** are very powerful computers used to do extremely complicated calculations.

Parallel jobs

Parallel computing or **parallel processing** means computing with a large number of *CPU** *chips** at the same time. Parallel computing is often used for jobs that deal with huge amounts of data. Parallel processors can work at a speed measured in *MIPS (Millions of Instructions Per Second)**. Parallel computers usually process groups, or **arrays**, of pieces of data (called **data elements**). They need a kind of *programming**, called **parallel programming** or **concurrent programming**.

SIMD (Single Instruction Multiple Data) parallel processing means the CPUs all do the same job on lots of data. **MIMD (Multiple Instruction Multiple Data)** means the different CPUs can do different jobs at the same time.

Data processing

A data processing department (see above) often has several sections, all connected to a mainframe (see above).

*In the **operations section**, **computer operators**, **data entry workers** or **keyboardists** input* data into the mainframe.*

Operations section

*Data is stored in a **data library**, usually on large tape cartridges*.*

Data library

Large, powerful processing unit

*In the **applications section**, **systems analysts** design new programs* and programmers* write them.*

Applications section

*At the **information section** or **help desk**, **support staff** give other users advice about how to use the system.*

Information section

*Technicians and **technical support staff** look after computer equipment and solve the more difficult software* problems.*

Maintenance section

Print section

*Mainframes often have a **print department**. Documents* are printed there, collected and returned to the users.*

Workstations

Workstation can mean the desk where you use your computer. But it also means a powerful type of computer. These workstations have their own *processing units** and are usually used by one person, but they can be linked together so that their power can be shared by many users across a *network**. They are often used for *computer-aided design** and can sometimes have very large, high-quality flat screens.

A type of workstation computer

Flat screen

Case

 ## Dedication

Dedicated or **special-purpose computers** are built to do just one job. **Dedicated word processors** and **electronic typewriters** are computers made just for writing, and *games computers** are just for playing games. Dedicated computers are good at what they do, but they often can't run new *programs**, so they go out of date quickly.

General-purpose computers are computers that aren't dedicated.

Dedicated word processor

 ## Other uses

These are some of the many ways computers are used in different areas of life.

• Lots of household items, such as video recorders and microwave ovens, are *computerized**. You *input** instructions by pressing buttons on a **control panel**. Your instructions are really a kind of short program.

Microwave oven   Control panel

• In shops, **cashless payment** or **EFTPOS (Electronic Funds Transfer at Point Of Sale) systems** let you pay for goods using a card. A computer reads details from a **magnetic strip** on your card, and uses network links to check the details with your bank's computer. Many shops also have **computerized checkouts**. Each item in the shop has a **UPC (Universal Product Code)**. A computer reads the code, shows the price and keeps a record of the things that are sold. **Visa® Cash** uses a *chip** embedded on a card, which stores monetary value. The card is used instead of cash. *Smart cards** have a similar function.

• **CAM (Computer-Aided Manufacturing)**, or **factory automation**, uses computers to control **robots** - machines that can do work instead of humans. **Hard automation** means the machines are dedicated (see left) and can do only one task. More complicated robots can be programmed to do a variety of different jobs. Some have **vision systems** and can "see" their

work using a camera. **Guided vehicle systems** are mobile robots that can find their way around a factory.

• To get into museums or underground stations, you often need a **computer-coded ticket**. This has a magnetic strip (see left) on the back containing coded information. You put the ticket into a special gate, where a computer reads the strip and opens the gate.

Magnetic strip

Computer-coded ticket

TOM'S TRAVEL & TRANSPORT
Valid for 1 journey

Not transferable

• **Touchscreens** are often used in museums and information centres. You can choose which information to see on the screen by pressing different parts of it.
• **Concept keyboards** are used in shops such as fast-food restaurants. Different items can be bought by pressing specific buttons.
• **Technological warfare** means using computers to make weapons more deadly. Modern missiles have computerized **electronic guidance systems** so that they can find their targets.
• **Computer-assisted therapy** means using computers to help people. For example, there is a *computer game** which teaches deaf children to pronounce words.
• **CAT (Computerized Axial Tomography) scanners** in hospitals use computers to make colour 3-D X-rays, or **CAT scans.** These show a very clear picture of the inside of parts of the body.

CAT scan of a hand

Peripherals

In computing, the word **peripheral** really means any piece of *hardware** apart from the computer's actual *processing unit**. But it is also used to mean an extra piece of hardware which you add to your *computer system** to do a particular job, such as extra *input and output devices**. A number of peripherals sold together is called a **kit** or a **bundle** - for example, you can buy a *multimedia bundle**, containing everything you need to run *multimedia** software**.

 ## Pointing devices

A type of peripheral called a **pointing device** allows you to point at and select options on the screen. An ordinary *mouse** is the most common kind, but there are lots of others. For example, a **long-distance mouse** is used to move a *pointer** on a large screen for showing something to an audience. Its long cable lets you stand away from the screen.

Some pointing devices are used for drawing and writing on the screen. A **graphics tablet** is a flat pad which you can write or draw on. The marks you make appear on the screen.

Long-distance mouse

Graphics tablet

 ## Game control

Joysticks are peripherals used to play computer *games**. A joystick has a steering stick set into a base, with **fire buttons** for shooting. An **autofire button** lets you fire continuously, without pressing again and again. Suction feet hold the joystick firmly to the table.

A **control pad** is like a joystick, but has no stick, only buttons.

Joystick

Top fire button

Steering stick

Fire buttons

Autofire button

Base

Suction foot

Lots of computer games involve flying an aircraft or a spacecraft. A **flightstick** is a special joystick made for flying games. A **flight yoke** is a larger device with a kind of steering wheel which you hold with both hands. A **flight console** is even bigger, and consists of a flight yoke with pedals.

 ## Scanners

A **scanner** or **image scanner** is a machine used to copy an image from paper into a computer. This is called **scanning in**. A device called a **scan head** inside the scanner bounces light off the image. The patterns of light are collected by **Charge Coupled Devices (CCDs)**. These send information about the image to the computer, which then recreates the image on the screen.

Most scanners can do **colour scans**, **monochrome** or **mono scans** (black and white), or **halftone scans** (different shades of grey).

• There are several kinds of **flatbed scanners.** You usually put the image on a piece of glass called a **scanner window**, and the scan head slowly moves across it.

Flatbed scanner

Scan head

Scanner window

• A **hand scanner** is useful for small images. You drag, or **track**, it slowly across the image. A special **scan mat** or **track pad** can be used to hold the image still.

Hand scanner

Image

• A **drum scanner** produces high-quality scans. The image is taped onto a cylinder or **drum**. The drum spins round very quickly while a scan head scans the image.

• **Mark scanners** are used to read questionnaires and multiple choice exam papers. The scanner reads which boxes have been ticked and the computer sorts out the results.

• **Optical Character Recognition (OCR)** scanners can scan written and printed *text**. A computer *program** recognizes the letters by **matrix matching** (comparing each letter shape to its own store of letters) or by **feature extraction** (analyzing the parts of each shape).

*Computer system, 4; Games, 42; Hardware, 4; Input and output devices, 6; Mouse, 7; Multimedia, 43; Multimedia bundle, 43; Pointer, 7; Processing unit, 8; Program, 44; Software, 4, 24; Text, 5

Carrying data

Cables, **leads** or **wires** link peripherals to your computer. **Connectors** on the ends of the cables plug into *ports** in the back of the *processing unit**, and into sockets in the peripherals they are connected to. They can also connect using **infra-red transmitters**, so that the peripheral has no cables. Ports and cables work in three main ways - **serial transmission**, **parallel transmission**, and *USB** **transmission**. Parallel and USB transmission can carry more data at a time.

Serial ports and **serial cables** can only carry, or **transmit**, one *bit** of data at a time. They are often used for

*mouses** and *modems**, which do not send much data at a time. An **RS-232 port** is a common kind of serial port.

A serial cable has two **data wires**, or **data lines**, for carrying data - one in each direction - and extra wires which carry other signals to control the transmission of the data.

Serial cable

Connector

Extra wires

Data wires

Parallel ports (often called **printer ports**) and **parallel cables** can transmit a whole *byte** (eight bits) of data at a time, along eight parallel wires

inside the cable. They are usually used for printers which need to receive a lot of data.

A parallel cable has eight data wires in each direction.

Parallel cable

Extra wires

Data wires   Connector

Data travelling in a cable can be damaged by **interference** caused by electricity from somewhere else. The longer a cable is, the worse the interference.

 ## Digital cameras

Digital camera

Ordinary cameras convert light into an image on a piece of film. **Digital cameras** convert light into *binary** data - information stored in a code made up of zeros and ones. A digital camera can be plugged into a *PC**, in order to *download** images in the camera's *memory** and see them on the screen. Images can be altered on the screen using *graphics software**. Some digital cameras can be directly connected to a *printer** or a television, to make viewing images easier.

Digital video cameras are used to *input** moving pictures in the same way. They are used for **video conferencing** or **teleconferencing**, where several people are linked together on a *network** or on the *Internet** and can see each other talking on their computer screens. Video conferencing can use **full motion** (high-quality) **video**, or **freeze frame video**, which is poorer quality but easier to send across a network.

Digital video cameras are also used to send video images via the Internet. This means that live video pictures from all over the world can be seen via the *World Wide Web**. Cameras which are set up like this are called **Web cameras** or **Web cams**.

Digital video camera

Digital cameras are also used to input images which can be processed by a computer to make *computer art**.

Home help

Home automation means using computers to control things such as light switches and heating. A peripheral called a **butler in a box** can be linked to a computer. It "hears" spoken instructions and sends signals to automatic devices around the house. It is very useful for disabled people.

Butler in a box

Computer networks

Networks link computers together so they can exchange information. On a network, you can send data to another computer in the same building, in a different town or on the other side of the world. You can send *text**, *graphics**, or any other kind of *computerized** information.

Sending data in this way is called **telecommunications** or **datacommunications**, often shortened to **telecomms**, **datacomms** or just **comms**. A computer that is on a network is said to be **networked**, **linked up**, **wired** or **online** (although *on line** can also mean switched on). A network within a single organization is often called an **intranet**, or an **extranet** if outside users can access it. It is protected from unauthorised users by a *program** called a **firewall**. Computers can be networked so that they can share resources, for example several computers may share a *printer**. Each computer is called a **client**, and they are linked via a server (see facing page). This is called **client-server technology**. A computer that is not on a network is often called a **standalone computer**.

LANs and WANs (see right) are the most common kinds of network. They are often linked to each other to make up more complicated networks. The *Internet**, for example, is a worldwide network made up of thousands of networks, including LANs and WANs, joined together.

 ## Passwords

Some networked computers have **password protection**. You have to type in a **password** – a secret word – before you are allowed to see the data. This stops people using the network to find, or **access**, secret data that is held on other computers. However, some people, called *hackers**, still manage to use networks to access secret data.

LANs

A **Local Area Network**, or **LAN**, links computers in the same room or building. Any piece of *hardware** linked to the LAN is called a **node**. Nodes can include printers, *scanners** and other *peripherals**, as well as the computers themselves. There are several kinds of LAN, including **token ring LANs**, **star LANs**, **bus LANs**, **snowflake LANs**, **optical LANs** and **ethernet LANs**. They have various kinds of layout, or **topology**.

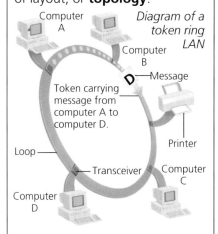

Diagram of a token ring LAN

Computer A

Computer B

Message

Token carrying message from computer A to computer D.

Loop

Printer

Transceiver

Computer C

Computer D

In a token ring LAN, the nodes are linked to a ring, or **loop**, of *cable**. Each node has a device called a **transceiver**, which sends and receives messages. An electronic signal, called a **token**, passes around the loop, picking up and delivering messages. Each message contains a code called an **address**, to make sure it is dropped off when it reaches the right node.

 ## WANs

Satellite

A **Wide Area Network**, or **WAN**, is a network that covers an area bigger than a LAN (see left). WANs can extend over long distances.

Some WANs use modems (see facing page) to send data over telephone wires. Messages can also be sent in the form of radio signals. These are beamed up to **communications satellites** in space, and sent back down to their destination.

 ## Network cables

Network systems use various kinds of cable. WANs usually use existing telephone wires, or **fibre optic cables**, which are now replacing them. These are made of **optical fibres** which use light instead of electricity to carry data.

Coaxial cable, sometimes used for LANs, is made up of two strands inside a wrapping called a **shield**. It can be **thick** (or **thicknet**), which is for carrying data a long way, or **thin** (also called **thinnet** or **cheapernet**) for short distances. Signals from one cable can *interfere** with another cable, damaging, or **corrupting**, the message. This interference is known as **crosstalk**.

Fibre optic cable

Modems

A **modem** (short for **MOdulate/ DEModulate**) allows computer data to be sent down a telephone line. Computers send data in the form of a series of pulses, known as **digital signals**. A modem converts, or **modulates**, these into **analog signals** (signals in the form of waves). At the other end, another modem has to **demodulate** (decode) the data back into digital signals so another computer can receive it.

How modems work

Computer sending message

Digital signal

Modem

Analog signal

Modem

Digital signal

Computer receiving message

Duplex transmission means a modem can carry data in two directions - both to and from your computer. A **full-duplex modem** can transmit in both directions at once. A **half-duplex modem** can only transmit in one direction at once. A **fax/ modem** allows data to be sent to a **facsimile** or **fax machine**, which prints it out on paper.

Modems come in various shapes and sizes. A **desktop** **modem** is a box about 15cm (6in) long, with a *cable** which plugs into a computer. A **portable modem** is much smaller and can be used with a *notebook** computer. These are both **external modems**. A **modem card**, or **internal modem**, is a kind of *expansion card** that fits inside the *processing unit**.

Desktop modem

The speed of a modem is measured in *bits** **per second** (**bps**). A fast modem sends data at about 56,000 bits per second. Some people call bps **baud rate**. In fact, baud rate is slightly different. It is a measurement of the number of waves per second in the analog signal (see left). Some modems *compress** *data** (arrange it so that it uses up less bits) to make transmission faster.

Modem card

A modem must be connected to a telephone line. A **dial-up modem** is used with an ordinary telephone line. A modem can be used with a special **leased line** instead, to keep it separate from the telephone line.

BABT-approved modems have been checked by the **British Approvals Board for Telecommunications**. A modem that is not BABT-approved is known as a **grey modem**.

An **ISDN** (**Integrated Services Digital Network**) line can carry *digital** data at a faster rate than a modem. A **terminal** (or **ISDN**) **adaptor** connects a computer to an ISDN line.

 ## Network words

• **Communication channel** A wire, *cable** or any kind of pathway that carries a message.
• **Bandwidth** The data-carrying capacity of a cable or any other communication channel, measured in bps (see left). A channel that can carry a lot of data has a **high bandwidth**.
• **Protocol** A system computers use to recognize each other and check data has been received. Also called **electronic etiquette** or **handshaking**.
• **Server** A computer that serves other computers on a network. A **file server** stores and organizes data that all the computers can use. A **net server** or **local server** links individual computers or small networks to big networks.
• **Mail** Messages sent to a computer over a network. (See *e-mail** and *Internet**.)
• **Packet-switching** A way of splitting large amounts of data into small sections, or **packets**, which can be sent across a network more easily. A **PAD** (**Packet Assembler and Disassembler**) *program** splits up the data and puts it together again at its destination.
• **Workgroup** A group of people, usually in an office, who work together using a computer network to share and swap data.
• **Bulletin Board System** (**BBS**) A networked computer which network users can access and leave messages on for other users to read. You can also **download**, or copy, *files**, such as programs and *graphics**, from a BBS.
• **Host** A networked computer, especially one that provides a service, such as a BBS (see above).

How computers work

Computers do all their calculations using a code made up of just two numbers - 0 and 1. This system is called **binary code**, or **binary**. When data is fed into a computer, it has to be converted into binary code. Information in binary code is often called **digital information**.

Bits and bytes

Each 0 or 1 is called a **bit** (short for **binary digit**). Bits usually travel around the computer in groups of eight, called **bytes**.

An example of a byte   One bit

`00111001`

The processing work in a computer is done by chips (see facing page). Electronic pathways called **buses** link the chips together, and carry data between them. Buses are used in three ways: **data buses** carry the data itself; **control buses** carry instructions telling the computer what to do with the data; and **address buses** tell the computer where in its *memory** to find or store data.

A simple bus is made up of eight *tracks**. Each track carries one bit, so the whole bus carries one byte. Bits travel in the form of electrical signals in the tracks. One kind of electrical signal represents a "1" bit. Another kind represents a "0" bit.

Diagram of à simple 8-bit bus

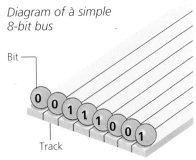

Bit

Track

Today, most buses have more than eight tracks so they can carry more data. A **16-bit bus** has 16 tracks and carries two bytes at a time. Some computers have a **32-bit bus** or even a **64-bit bus**.

A **multiplexed bus** is a bus which can carry more than one bit on each track, using a kind of technology called **time division multiplexing**.

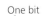
Buses and cards

As well as linking the chips (see facing page) in a computer, buses also contain *expansion slots**. These are slots into which you can put *expansion cards**. There are several makes and types of bus, and you can only use a particular expansion card if you have the right type of bus to put it into.

The first *IBM PC** had a 16-bit bus known as the **AT bus** or the **expansion bus**, because it was the first bus with expansion slots. This type of bus became the standard, and was soon known as the **ISA (Industry Standard Architecture) bus**. The ISA bus is not very fast, but it is still popular, because lots of expansion cards are made to fit it.

Newer kinds of bus have been developed which work much faster, such as the **MCA (Micro Channel Architecture) bus** and the **EISA (Extended ISA) bus**. These are both 32-bit buses. The EISA bus is more popular, as it is **backwardly compatible** - it can hold the older ISA cards as well as its own EISA cards.

A **local bus** is a different, faster bus system that links the *CPU** chip to the *RAM** chips. Since the *386** computer appeared, *PCs** have had both types of bus - a main bus (either

ISA, EISA or MCA) and a local bus. Expansion cards can be fitted into both types.

A diagram of the two-bus system

Key: Main bus   Local bus

Local bus expansion slots

CPU chip

RAM chips

Other chips

Main bus expansion slots

The local bus can only hold special **local bus expansion cards**. There are two main types of local bus, each with its own type of card. The **VESA (Video Electronics Standard Association) local bus**, also called the **VL-bus**, is the usual type, and most local bus expansion cards are made to fit it. There is also a faster, but more expensive, type of local bus called the **PCI (Peripheral Component Interconnect) local bus**.

*Notebook** PCs often have **PCMCIA (Personal Computer Memory Cards International Association) expansion cards** which are small and light, like credit cards. The notebook's VESA or PCI bus is specially adapted to hold these.

PCMCIA card

*386 computer, 12: CPU, 9; Expansion card, 8; Expansion slot, 8; IBM PC, 12; Memory, 22; Notebook, 13; PC, 4, 12; RAM, 22; Track, 8

Chips

Chips (also called **microchips, silicon chips** and **Integrated Circuits** or **ICs**) do the processing work inside a computer. Each chip does a particular job, such as storing or organizing data. The main chip in a computer is the *CPU**, which does calculations on data.

A chip is made of a tiny slice, or **wafer**, of a substance called **silicon**. The wafer is covered with thousands of electronic pathways, arranged in layouts called *circuits**.

Each chip is protected by a plastic case, or **housing**, with wires called **feet** connecting the chip to the computer.

A chip in its plastic housing

Protective housing

Wire foot

A chip without its housing

Circuits

Silicon base

Part of a chip's surface, hundreds of times bigger than in real life.

The *architecture** of a CPU chip is very important. A **CISC (Complex Instruction Set Computer) CPU** has complicated architecture and can follow many different kinds of instructions. A **RISC (Reduced Instruction Set Computer) CPU** has simpler architecture. It follows fewer instructions, but runs faster than a CISC CPU.

 # How chips work

Silicon, which forms the base of a chip, is a **semiconductor** - it can carry some electricity. The circuits covering the silicon base are made of different kinds of semiconductor. When a chip is built, the different semi-conductors are made to cross each other in certain ways, to form tiny devices called **transistors**. Bits (see facing page) pass through these transistors and are changed from 1s into 0s, or vice versa. This is how processing happens.

The transistors are arranged in patterns, or **configurations**, so that they can perform different *functions**, such as adding or comparing numbers. A simple arrangement of transistors is called a **logic gate**. There are several types. The commonest is a **nand gate**. The other types include **nor gates, and gates, or gates** and **not gates**. Arrangements of logic gates make up **flip-flops**, such as **JK-type flip-flops** and **D-type flip-flops**.

Flip-flops and logic gates are very complicated and much too small to see in real life, but they can be represented using diagrams called **logic symbols**.

A logic symbol diagram of a logic gate

A logic symbol diagram of a D-type flip-flop

(***?) **Computer words**

• **Word** A group of bytes travelling on the same bus.
• **Floating point arithmetic** A way of processing very large or small numbers. The computer converts these numbers into formulae, such as as "23e-80", which are easier for it to store and work on. Normal computer arithmetic is called **fixed point arithmetic**.

• **MIPS (Millions of Instructions Per Second)** A measure of simple **processing speed** (the speed at which a computer can do calculations).
• **FLOPS (FLoating point Operations Per Second)** A measure of processing speed when **floating point operations** (calculations done using floating point arithmetic) are being used. A million FLOPS is called a **megaflop**, and a billion FLOPS is

called a **gigaflop**. These units are used to measure fast, complicated mathematical calculations on big computers.
• **Maths co-processor** An extra CPU chip, built into most computers, and used for mathematical calculations.
• **Clock doubling** A kind of technology that makes the CPU run twice as fast as the computer's *clock**. This makes the computer run faster.

Memory and storage

Memory, which is made up of *chips**, and **storage devices**, such as disks (see facing page), hold *data** (information) that computers use. The main difference between them is that memory mostly holds data you are using when your computer is switched on, and storage devices hold data you need to keep when you switch your computer off. This data includes *software** and *files**.

When you want to use a piece of software or open a file, you transfer it from a storage device into the memory. This is called **loading**. Transferring data from the memory back onto a storage device is called **saving**.

This diagram shows how memory and storage devices are used.

Memory

You load data into the memory when you need to use it.

Data

You save data on storage devices to keep it safe when you switch the computer off.

Data

Storage devices

The amount of data a memory chip or storage device can hold is called its **capacity**. Capacity is measured in *bytes**. A **kilobyte**, **Kbyte**, **KB** or **K** is 1024 bytes. A **megabyte**, also called a **Mbyte**, **MB** or **meg**, is 1024 kilobytes (about a million bytes). A **gigabyte**, **Gbyte**, **GB** or **gig** is 1024 megabytes.

RAM

RAM (Random-Access Memory) is the largest part of your computer's memory. It holds the data which you load into your computer when you want to use it (see left). RAM is **volatile** - when you switch the computer off, the data in RAM disappears. RAM is called "Random-Access Memory" because it takes the computer the same amount of time (called the **access time**) to find, or **access**, any part of a RAM chip. An average *PC** has about 64 megabytes (see left) of RAM.

The most common type of RAM, called **Dynamic RAM** or **DRAM**, holds data in the form of electrical energy. A DRAM chip contains thousands of tiny electronic devices called **capacitors** or **buckets**. Each bucket can store one *bit** (either a 1 or a 0 - the smallest unit of data a computer can hold). A capacitor can either be empty (an **empty bucket**), representing a 0, or filled up with electricity (a **full bucket**), representing a 1.

A group, or **array**, of eight buckets is called a **cell** or a **memory location**. Each cell has an **address** which the computer uses to find the data.

Static RAM is another kind of RAM. It has a faster access time than DRAM, but also costs more.

In most computers, there is also a small amount of **CMOS (Complementary Metal Oxide Semiconductor) RAM**, which keeps information such as the time and the date. It has a **RAM battery** which **refreshes** the RAM (keeps it going) while the computer is switched off, so it does not lose its data.

The most frequently used data from RAM is kept in the **cache memory**, or **cache**. This is an extra-fast RAM chip in between the main RAM chips and the *CPU**. The CPU can find data from the cache much faster than from main RAM.

Extra RAM

You can enlarge or **expand** your RAM with extra RAM *chips**, which are arranged in rows called **SIMMs** (**Single In-line Memory Modules**). You can also buy *expansion cards** which contain extra RAM. Another way to expand RAM is to use **shadow RAM** or **virtual RAM**. This breaks the data into pieces called **segments** and **pages**, and stores some of them on your hard disk (see facing page) to make more space in RAM. Using shadow RAM can make a computer work slowly.

ROM

ROM stands for **Read-Only Memory**. It holds the basic instructions a computer needs to start working when you switch it on, and to control the way it works. Unlike RAM, ROM is **non-volatile** - it never loses its data. The data is held in the arrangements of the wires in ROM chips, and cannot be changed. ROM is called Read-Only Memory because you can only "read" it, not change, or "rewrite" it. However, some computers have a bit of **Erasable Programmable ROM**, or **EPROM**, which you can change and update.

Firmware is a kind of ROM which contains software. Sometimes the *operating system** is held on firmware in your computer when you buy it.

Storage devices

Storage devices, such as disks and tapes, hold data and keep it safe while it is not being used. This is sometimes called **secondary storage**. **Internal storage devices** are inside your computer's *processing unit**, and **external storage devices** are separate from the computer. A device called a **drive** is used to **read from** (collect data from) a disk or tape, or **write to** it (add new data).

Floppy disks

Floppy disks, also called **magnetic disks** or **floppies**, are external storage devices, made of flexible (but not really floppy) plastic. Data is stored as arrangements of tiny magnetic particles on the disk's surface.

Floppy disks come in various sizes, such as **3.5 inch** and **5.25 inch**. 3.5 inch floppy disks, also called **diskettes**, **microfloppies**, or **minifloppies**, are the most common, and have a capacity (see facing page) of up to 2.88 megabytes (see facing page) of data. Floppy disks can be used to keep **back-ups** (spare copies) of your data and for carrying data to a different computer.

3.5 inch floppy disk

- Window
- Disk guard
- Plastic case
- Disk hub

A floppy disk fits into a computer's **floppy disk drive**. The drive spins the disk while a **read/write head** reads its data, or writes new data onto it.

Floppy disk drive

Read/write head

Disk case with disk inside

The hard disk

The **hard disk** is an internal storage device which stays permanently inside a **hard disk drive** in a computer. Hard disks work in the same way as floppies, but they are made of metal and can hold much more data. (A hard disk in a *PC** usually holds up to about 500 megabytes.) Most people use their hard disk to keep all their *software** and *files** organized in a convenient way.

Storage words

- **Data compression** Using a *program** to rewrite data so that it takes up less space.
- **Tape cartridge** or **data cartridge** A storage device which holds data on magnetic tape. It uses a **tape drive**, **deck** or **transport**. Cartridges are often used to keep back-ups. A **SyQuest cartridge** can hold 1.5GB (see facing page) of data.
- **Zip drive** A drive which can store 100MB on a **zip disk**.
- **Jaz drive** A drive which can store 2GB on a **jaz disk**.
- **SCSI drive** (pronounced "scuzzy drive") A drive which connects to a PC using a *SCSI**.
- **Disk cache** A device which stores the most frequently used data from the hard disk, so that the computer can find it quickly.
- **Density** The amount of data a storage device can hold on a given area of its surface. **High density 3.5 inch disks** have more capacity (see facing page) than **double density** ones.
- **Formatting** The surface of a disk is **formatted**, or prepared for use, by being divided into areas called **tracks** and **sectors**. The computer uses these to find the right part of a disk quickly.

Optical discs

Optical discs (always spelt disc, not disk) are a kind of storage device with a very high capacity (see facing page). **Compact discs** or **CDs** are the most common kind. A CD can hold 680 megabytes of data - over 200 times more than a floppy (see above). Most CDs used in computers are *CD-ROMs**, which the user can read from, but not write to (see above). They are often used for *multimedia* software**. **WORM (Write Once Read Many) discs** can be written onto once by the user, but can be read lots of times. **Erasable optical discs**, also called **magneto-optical**, **floptical discs**, or **rewritable discs**, can be written onto many times.

An optical disc usually stores data as a pattern of holes, called **pits**, and flat areas, called **lands**, on its surface. It is read by an **optical disc drive**, which shines a *laser beam** at the disc. The laser light is reflected off the lands and the pits in different ways. The drive reads the data by collecting patterns of reflected light.

Close-up of part of a CD-ROM

Land

Pit

Software

In order to do anything useful, a computer needs instructions. These instructions are called **software**, and there are many different kinds.

Software is usually kept on *storage devices**, such as *disks**, when it is not being used, and loaded into a computer's *RAM** when it is needed. Software is always written in the form of *programs** (sets of instructions for doing particular things).

A computer is nearly always using, or **running**, several programs at once, on different levels. Most computers use three software levels.

Diagram showing software levels

Applications

Utility

Operating system

Systems

Systems software runs a computer's basic *functions**, such as controlling which programs are running at any one time. **Utility software** helps you organize your data. This is known as **housekeeping**. It also includes programs called **drivers** which control, or **drive**, devices that are linked to the computer, such as the *printer**. **Applications software** programs, also called **applications**, let you do specific jobs such as writing, drawing or doing calculations.

Systems and utility software together make up the operating system (see right). This is usually already in a computer when you buy it. Applications software can be bought separately.

The OS

An **Operating System**, or **OS**, is a set of programs that control and organize everything the computer does, and provide a "background" for any other software that is being used. The operating system runs all the time, while other software runs "within" it or "on top of" it. The operating system includes the user interface (see below).

Most home *PCs** use an operating system called *Microsoft® Windows®** 95 or 98. This makes your PC easier to use. In business, **Windows® NT** is often used. Many older PCs use **MS-DOS®** (or just **DOS**), short for **Microsoft®Disk Operating System** (because it was originally just used to run *disk drives**). Other operating systems include **OS/2**, an operating system specially designed to do *multitasking**, and **UNIX**, a powerful operating system used on *workstations**. *Macs** have their own operating system, called **Mac OS**. The latest version of this is **Mac OS8**.

User interfaces

The **User Interface** or **UI** is a part of the operating system (see above). It lets you communicate with, or hold a **dialogue** with, your computer. It usually consists of screens which let you choose from a range of options. A **dialogue box** is a box which appears on the screen containing a particular choice or question about what you want to do.

Do you want to save this file?

Yes   No

A dialogue box which helps you save* data.

• A **menu-driven user interface** shows a list, or **menu**, of options, across the top of the screen, in a panel called a **menu bar**. When you choose one, another menu called a **pull-down menu** drops below the bar, offering you a further list of options to choose from.

• A **GUI** (**Graphical User Interface**) uses little pictures called **icons** to represent some of the options it offers you. You select the icon you want using the *mouse** or *keyboard**. GUIs are easy to use and are sometimes called **WIMP** (*Windows**, **Icons, Mouse and** *Pointer**) **interfaces**. Most GUIs also use *text** and menus to ask you questions and explain things.

These icons are from Intellipoint®, a program that lets you control the way your mouse works.

• With a **3-D user interface**, you can use your mouse to move, or **navigate**, around a 3-D world in computer space, or **digital space**. For example, the screen might show a 3-D view of a street and buildings. If you wanted to send an *e-mail** message, you would choose the post office. This kind of user interface is sometimes called a **desktop metaphor** - a computer imitation of the real world.

Files

When you use software, you often create pieces of data, which you want to keep. A piece of data like this is called a **file**. A **data file** contains data such as *text**, numbers or *graphics**. A data file containing mainly text is called a **text file** or **document**. A **program file** (also called an **executable**) holds a *program** which is used to work on data.

When you make a file, you give it a name, or **filename**. For example, in DOS (see facing page), filenames have two parts, separated by a dot. The **identifier** (before the dot) describes the data in the file. The **file extension** (after the dot) shows what kind of file it is.

Parts of a DOS filename

These are some of the DOS file extensions you might see:
• **.txt** A text file
• **.sys** A file containing systems software (see facing page)
• **.exe** An executable (a name for a program file). A **.com** file is another type of executable file.

Most operating systems (see facing page) have a **file manager**, a program which shows you a list of your files and helps you organize them into groups called **directories** or **folders** and **sub-directories**. Windows 95 (see facing page) has a file manager program called **Windows Explorer**.

Part of a file manager
— Directory for letters
— Sub-directory for letters to Lisa
— Files containing letters to Lisa

You **open** a file to start working on it, and to finish, you **close** it. You have to *save** a file before closing it, if you want to keep everything you have done. You can **move** files around in the file manager, **copy** files between your *hard disk** and *floppy disks**, and **delete** or **erase** (remove) files.

 ## Packages

A piece of applications software is called a **software package**. A package containing several applications is called **integrated software** or a **software suite**. Software can be **custom-written** (written specially for your needs) or **shrinkwrapped** (mass-produced). **Bundled software** is software sold with a computer.

A software package usually comes in a box containing floppy disks and **documentation** (booklets), including a handbook or **manual**, which explains how to install and use the software.

A typical software package

Box
Manual
Other information
Disks

Software can also be copied, or *downloaded**, from one computer to another, if they are *networked**. You can often get **freeware** (free software) in this way. **Shareware** (also called **honourware**) is similar, but you may have to pay to use it.

 ## Installing

You usually **install** applications software (see facing page), or transfer it from *CD-ROM**, floppy disks or the *Internet** onto your hard disk, so that you can find it easily. When you want to use an application, you *load** it. This transfers it into your computer's *memory**. There are many different applications for playing *games**, learning, and lots of other things.

Screen showing games software

Screen showing graphics software

Computer-Aided Design (CAD)*

*CAD, 35; CD-ROM, 43; Downloading, 19; Floppy disk, 23; Games, 42; Graphics, 36; Hard disk, 23; Internet, 28; Loading, 22; Memory, 22; Network, 18; Program, 44; Saving, 22; Text, 5

25

Basic applications

Most computers come with a set of basic *applications* software**, or **core applications**. These enable you to do everyday tasks, such as writing, doing calculations, and keeping lists of data. The computer may also come with an *operating system**, such as *DOS**.

You can only use an application if it is in the right **format** - designed to work with your operating system. For example, if you use DOS with Microsoft Windows (see below), you can only use applications that are designed specifically "**for Windows**".

Microsoft Windows

Microsoft Windows® is a well-known operating system which works with *PCs**. It uses rectangular areas of the screen, called **windows**, to display data. One window can take up the whole screen, or several smaller windows can be displayed at once, each one running a different application such as a word processor (see below) or database (see facing page). You can easily swap from one window to another. A window can be **maximized** (made as big as possible), **minimized** (made as small as possible), or **iconified** (made into a picture, or *icon**).

Word processing

A **Word Processing** (**WP**) *program**, is a type of software that helps you write letters, stories and any other kind of *text**. You can change or **edit** your piece of writing, or *document**, as much as you like. Some word processing words are listed here.

• **WYSIWYG** (**What You See Is What You Get**) display, pronounced "wizziwig". This means that the document looks the same on the screen as it does when you print it out.

• **Word wrap** This means that when you get to the end of a line, the next word automatically appears on the line below.

• **Hyphenation** Putting hyphens into the text. Some WP programs do this automatically.

• **Page layout** The way text is arranged on the page. You can set **margins** (borders at the edges of the page) and **headers** and **footers** (separate pieces of text, such as page numbers, at the top and bottom of the page).

• **Tab** (short for **tabulate**) This *function** lets you preset different margins, so you can set out data in columns and rows easily.

• **Justified text** Text that lines up on both the left-hand side and the right-hand side.

• **Block** A piece of text. You can choose a block of text and **cut and paste** it (move it to another part of the document or another file), or **copy** it (repeat it).

Screen showing word-processed text

• **Formatting text** Changing the appearance of the text. For example, text can be **bold**, **underlined** or *italic*.

• **Typeface** or **font** The style of the **type** (letters and numbers). There are thousands of different fonts, such as **Times**, **Helvetica**, Casablanca Antique, Kids, and Vîkîng.

• **Point size** or **type size** The height of the type. A **point** is $1/72$ of an inch. This sentence is written in 10.5 point text.

• **Spellcheck** This checks your spelling and suggests several replacements for any words it doesn't recognize.

• **Wordcount** This counts the words in your document.

• **Search and replace** This function lets you change a particular word (for example a name) into another word, throughout the text.

• **TWP** (**Technical Word Processor**) A word processing program made for writing technical or scientific data, such as mathematical formulae.

Margin — Header — "Palatino" typeface — Selected block

Communication

Communication is the act of sending out messages or signals to make known a fact, express a feeling and so on. Animals communicate for many reasons such as to attract mates, deter predators, show fear or to keep in contact with others.

Visual signals travel faster than sound, but most can only be seen over short distances. As in **humans**, an animal's *body posture* can signal different moods.

Page 8   **Wordcount:71**

Footer — Italic text — Underlined text — Bold text — "Gill sans" typeface — Wordcount

Financial software

Businesses often use **financial** or **business** *software** to do calculations on finances (money).

Using a spreadsheet (see right)

There are several different kinds of financial software:

• **Personal financial management software** This keeps records of your private spending.

• **Business accounting software** Software that helps businesses keep financial records and organize wages and tax.

• **Financial analysis software** This is used by banks and businesses to examine financial data and predict, or forecast, future profits and spending.

Most financial software *programs** use **spreadsheets** or **worksheets**. These are mathematical tables which show figures in horizontal **rows** and vertical **columns**.

Part of a spreadsheet Label Cell pointer

	Oct	Nov	Dec
Clothes	32.50	74.96	40.45
Going out	40.05	24.55	**55.40**
Bus fares	24.50	19.10	30.00
Total	97.05	118.61	125.85

Label   Value   Calculated cell

The title of a column or row is called a **label**. The information named by one label is called a **range** (for example, all the figures in the "Clothes" row). A single box in a spreadsheet is called a **cell**. You use the *mouse** or *keyboard** to move a **cell pointer**. This highlights one cell at a time so that you can write or change the number (called a **value**) in the cell.

A spreadsheet can also have **calculated cells**. These automatically add up the values in each row or column, and automatically change when you change the values. You can change the information in just one cell, row or column (a **local change**) or change the values for the whole spreadsheet (a **global change**).

 ## Databases

Database or **databank** *software** is used to manage databases - stores of information. It helps you find the data you want quickly and easily. For example, a club might use a database to keep a list of all its members. A **File Processing System** (**FPS**) is software for working with simple databases. A **DataBase Management System** (**DBMS**) is more powerful and can analyze data in lots of ways.

Each type of data in a database is called a **field** - for example, names, addresses and so on. A single piece of data is called an **entry**. Some databases help you to enter details by giving you a **form**, a screen where you fill in a collection of entries, called a **record**, about one particular thing. The way the fields and records are organized is called the **data hierarchy**. Some databases are very complicated, with hundreds of fields and millions of records. A **multimedia** *database has **visual data** (pictures) as well as *text**.

A **search** *function** can find particular entries in a database, and a **sort function** can sort out data into different orders, such as alphabetical order. A **filter function** sorts data into groups - for example, you could use a filter to make a list of all the people in one town or city.

Databases are also used in other ways. A **videotex system**, such as Teletext, uses a database to store information such as television schedules or weather forecasts. You can see the data on your television screen, using a remote control **keypad** (a small *keyboard**) to change from one **page** (screen of data) to another.

Businesses use **data warehousing** - accessing various databases to build up a picture of business conditions. A **data mart** does this for single subjects or departments.

A **medical expert system** (sometimes called a **medical jukebox**) uses a database to hold large amounts of medical information. Doctors use it to help diagnose illnesses.

A form showing data about a member of a club

The Internet

The **Internet**, also known as the **Net**, is a worldwide computer *network** made up of smaller networks. It offers various services, or **Internet facilities**, to anyone who is connected to it, or "**wired**". You can use the Net to send letters, talk to friends, copy *files** and *software** from other computers, and look up information from sources all over the world. The imaginary space you travel around in when you use the Net is called **cyberspace**. Even though you stay in one place, you make a "**virtual journey**" around the world by linking up to different places.

The Internet grew out of an American military network called **DARPANET** (**Defence Advanced Research Projects Agency NETwork**), which was then changed to **ARPANET**. This proved to be so useful that a new network, **NSFNET** (**National Science Foundation NETwork**), was created for research and educational organizations to use. By 1990, anyone could join, and the Internet was born. The Net is not strictly controlled, but the NSF recommends a set of rules for users, called the **acceptable use policy**.

This diagram shows the main connections on the NSFNET on a map of the USA.

 Connections

Any computer that is connected to the Internet is known as a **host**, and a network (a *LAN** or *WAN**) connected to the Net is called a **site**. Some sites, especially government and university networks, have a **leased line**. This is a permanent connection - the site is linked to the Net all the time.

If you are not on a leased line, you can access the Net by paying a company called an **Internet Service Provider (ISP)** or **Internet Access Provider (IAP)** to connect you. You can be connected in various ways:
- **Dial-in connection** This means the company has a direct link to the Internet. Using a *modem** or *terminal adaptor**, you dial in and use their connection.
- **Dial-up** or **terminal connection** With this type of connection, you connect to a company that does not have a direct link. Instead, their network is connected to the Net through a *computer system** called a **gateway**.
- **Digital connection** A direct link between a company and the Internet, through a **cable modem** (a fast modem linked to a *digital** line), or ISDN line.

- **Mail-only connection** A connection you can only use for e-mail (see below).

Data is transmitted over the Net using **protocols**, such as **TCP/IP** (**Transmission Control Protocol/Internet Protocol**). A protocol is a way of splitting data into chunks called **data packets**, or enclosing it in pieces of electronic code called "**envelopes**", so it travels safely to the right place.

 E-mail

E-mail, sometimes spelled **email**, is short for **electronic mail** - sending messages on the Internet. Most people use e-mail to send letters more cheaply and quickly than "**snail mail**", or normal mail. You can also e-mail *graphics** or *sound** files by attaching them to an e-mail message using a system called **MIME** (**Multi-purpose Internet Mail Extensions**). The standard e-mail protocol is called **SMTP** (**Simple Mail Transfer Protocol**).

Each person on the Internet has an **e-mail address** for sending and receiving e-mail. This consists of a **username** (the person's name), followed by an @ symbol (which means "at"), followed by the address. The address usually shows the country and the **domain** or **subdomain**, the place where the person can be found. There may also be a code showing the type of site (see left), such as **co** or **com** (a commercial site), **edu** or **ac** (academic), **gov** (government), or **org** (an organization).

An imaginary e-mail address

anna@usborne.co.uk

Username Domain   Code Country

Computer system, 4; Digital, 4; File, 25; Graphics, 36; ISDN, 19; LAN, 18; Modem, 19; Network, 18; Software, 4, 24; Sound, 40; Terminal adaptor, 19; WAN, 18

Using e-mail

To use e-mail (see facing page) you will need an **e-mail client program***. Some ISPs (see facing page) provide their own e-mail *software**. One popular program is called **Microsoft® Outlook™**. Other programs, such as **Eudora**, can be downloaded for free from the Net.

In most e-mail programs, you type the message into a *window** like the one shown below.

An e-mail composition window

Address Subject of message

Message

To send an e-mail, you type in the e-mail address of the person you are sending it to. You fill in the subject of the message, and then type in the message itself. You will need to be *online** to send the message.

An **e-mail header** is a piece of technical information at the top of an e-mail message, showing what route the message has taken. If an e-mail **bounces**, or fails to get through, it is sent back to you, and you can look at the header to see what went wrong. An **online directory** is a computer list of e-mail addresses.

 ## Newsgroups

Many people use the Internet to get in touch with people with the same interests, or to find out about particular subjects, through **newsgroups**, also called **discussion groups**. The main network for doing this is **Usenet**. It contains lots of groups, for all sorts of interests and hobbies.

Newsgroups are all named according to their subjects, called **topics** and **subtopics**. Topics include **comp** (computers), **sci** (science), **soc** (social groups), **rec** (recreation) and **alt** (alternative groups).

An imaginary name for a newsgroup about frogs

Topic Subtopics

If you want to use newsgroups you will need a program called a **newsreader**. Sometimes this is provided with *browser** software. For example, the *Netscape Communicator** package includes a newsreader called **Netscape Collabra**. Other programs, such as **Free Agent**, can be downloaded for free from the Net.

In a newsgroup, you can write, or **post**, messages or **postings**, and then see other people's answers appear on your screen, as well as corresponding one-to-one. Messages responding to an original posting are called **followups**. Lots of people can take part at once. **Flaming**, or sending **flame mail**, means sending angry messages. A **flame war** is an argument.

Most newsgroups have a **FAQ**

(Frequently Asked Questions) message for new members to read. This may be in the form of a posting, or it may appear on a *Web page**. This gives basic information about the group and the subject, which saves the other members having to answer the same questions over and over again.

Smileys (often spelt **smilies**), or **emoticons**, are little pictures made up from *characters** on the *keyboard**. They can be used to add emotions or extra meanings to your newsgroup messages. Here are some smileys. (You have to look at them sideways.)

:-) *Happy/sarcastic*

:-D *Laughing*

:-(*Sad/angry*

:-O *Surprised*

 ## Downloading files

Ftp (**file transfer protocol**) is the system you use to copy *files** from another computer onto your own, over the Internet. This is done using an **ftp program**. An **ftp site** is a site (see facing page) where files are available for downloading. You often need permission or **authorized access** to download a file, but there are lots of **anonymous ftp sites**, where files are freely available to anyone. Most browsers are capable of *downloading** from ftp sites, but are slower than ftp programs.

*Browser, 30; Character, 6; Downloading, 19; File, 25; Keyboard, 6; Netscape Communicator, 30; Online, 18; Program, 44; Software, 4, 24; Web page, 30; Window, 26

29

The World Wide Web

The **World Wide Web**, also called **WWW** or the **Web**, is an *Internet** facility that lets you look at information from all over the world. It is the most popular part of the Internet and stores a huge amount of information.

Web pages are information *documents** on the Web. Every Web page has its own address, called a **URL** (**Uniform Resource Locator**). All Web pages start with **http://** which stands for **hypertext transfer protocol**. This is the method that browsers (see right) use to read Web pages. The next part of the address shows the *domain** name. This is similar to an *e-mail address**. URLs may have a final section which gives the name of the page.

An imaginary URL

http://www.usborne.com/
index.html

Page title   Domain   Code

Web pages are *hypertext**-**linked**. This means that some words or pictures are "**live**": when you *click** on them with your *mouse**, they take you to other pages which could be located on a *server** thousands of miles away. Links which are live are called **hyperlinks**.

A hyperlink which has not been clicked on is called an **active link**. It is often, but not always, underlined. When you have visited the linked page, the link will normally change colour. It is then called a **followed link**. Pictures can also be hyperlinks.

Web sites

A set of Web pages belonging to a single organization is called a **Web site**. Some Web sites have a page which introduces the site. This is called an **entry page**. Most sites have a page which links to the other main areas of the site. This is called a **home page**. Some sites have a page which shows the layout of the entire site. This is called a **site map**.

There are Web sites about almost any subject. All sorts of organizations have sites, from businesses to schools, governments to individual users. Web sites are used to go shopping *online**, to find out the latest news, to play games, and to pass on information.

Different types of Web site

A government site

A bookstore site

A site about space

 Browsers

When you look at Web pages, you are **browsing** or "**surfing the Net**". Web pages are viewed using a *program** called a **browser**. The most widely-used browsers are **Microsoft® Internet Explorer** and **Netscape Navigator®**, which is combined with other Internet programs in a package called **Netscape Communicator®**. These find and display Web pages. Browsers contain many features to help you use the Web. Most browsers work in a similar way.

A program's controls appear on its **toolbar**. With a browser this is at the top of the *window**. While you browse the Web, you can look at Web pages using the **navigation buttons** on the toolbar.

The Microsoft Internet Explorer toolbar showing some of the navigation buttons

Stop   Home   History

Back   Refresh   Favorites

The **Back button** takes you back to the the last page you looked at. If you click on the **History button**, you will see a list of sites you have visited recently. Some sites are constantly being updated. The **Refresh** or **Reload button** *downloads** the page you are viewing again, so that you can see if it has changed. If a page is taking too long to download, you can use the **Stop button** to end the process.

You can keep track of sites you like using **Favorites** (also called **bookmarks** or **short cuts**). The browser contains a bookmarks *menu** in which you can store the addresses of sites you like. A browser can be set to display any Web page when it is started up. This page is called a **start-up page**, **home page** or **default page**.

Browsers save Web pages in a folder called the **cache**. This enables a browser to display a previously-viewed page more quickly, because it does not have to be downloaded again.

Clicking, 7; Documents, 25; Domain, 28; Downloading, 19; E-mail address, 21; Hypertext, 43; Internet, 28; Menu, 24; Mouse, 7; Online, 18; Program, 44; Server, 19; Window, 26

🌐 Web searching

The Web contains an enormous variety of information, and new pages (see facing page) are being added all the time. There is no central organization, which means that pages can be hard to find.

There are a number of *programs** located on sites (see facing page) which can be used to find pages on the Web. These programs are called **search engines**. There are two types of search engine. A **directory** classifies different pages, so that you can search using the subject matter of the page you want to find. An **index** enables a search by specific words, or **keywords**, related to the information on the page. In practice most search engines use a combination of both types.

Yahoo! is a directory.

AltaVista is an index.

Creating pages

Web pages are written as text *documents**. To turn a piece of text into a Web page, you have to add a *code** called **HTML**, or **HyperText Mark-Up Language**. This consists of commands called **tags** which are placed around pieces of *text** to tell a browser (see facing page) how to display text or *graphics**.

Web pages can either be created by adding tags to text using a *text editor**, or by using a program called a **Web editor**. Web editors enable you to design a page without writing HTML. Most of them work using a *WYSIWYG** display.

This sequence of tags will create a basic Web page.

```
                Page title
<HTML>
<HEAD>
<TITLE>My page</TITLE>
</HEAD>
<BODY>The text on your
page.</BODY>
</HTML>
                The information
                to be displayed
                goes here.
```

A page displayed in a Web editor

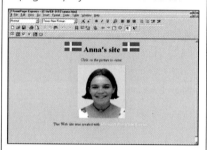

The text and tags which make up a Web page are called its **source**. The source for any page can be viewed by *clicking** an option in the browser's *menu**.

Some of the source for the Yahoo! page shown at the top of this page

Hyperlinks (see facing page), graphics or *sounds** can be added to pages, as well as background colours or patterns.

Many Web pages feature animations or images that perform an action when clicked on. These are often created by small programs called **applets**, in a *programming language** called *Java**. This helps to make the Web more useful, because pages can perform extra functions, such as featuring *pull-down menus** (menus which appear when you click on part of the page) and mathematical calculations.

This game was created using Java, and can be played on the Web.

〰️ Plug-ins

Programs called **plug-ins** enable browsers to use features on Web pages such as video images, radio broadcasts and interactive games. Useful plug-ins include **Flash Shockwave**, **RealPlayer™** and **QuickTime**. These can normally be *downloaded** from the *Internet** for free.

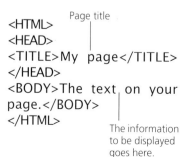

Other Internet features

Meeting places

There are a variety of ways to meet new people and chat to them using the *Internet** or *Net**. **IRC** or **Internet Relay Chat** is a system which allows you to type messages to people and see their responses straight away. It is organized into **chat rooms**: each room appears in a separate *window**. The window shows the **nicknames** (the names people choose while they are using IRC) of all the people in the room. One IRC *program** is **mIRC**, which you can *download** from the Net for free.

There are also other chat programs which allow users to meet in *Virtual Reality** settings, or *virtual worlds**. These allow users to choose what they look like on the screen. The image which represents a person is called an **avatar**. Some programs allow you to hear people actually speaking.

Avatars from a chat program

A chat room in a virtual world

You can keep track of whether people are *online** using **ICQ** ("**I seek you**"). This is a program which alerts you when people have come online and when they go **off-line**, or stop using the Internet. It also allows you to chat, or send *files**, to people.

Mailing lists

Mailing lists are a type of Internet discussion group. Members discuss topics by exchanging *e-mails**. Each message sent via the list gets sent to all the other members. There are mailing lists about a huge variety of subjects. If you are a member of a busy list, you may receive lots of messages every day. Each mailing list is run by a person, or a program called a **listserv**.

Push channels

Push channels are parts of a *browser** which regularly download up-to-date information. A variety of organizations offer their own services, such as news, weather and television listings, which can appear on your screen. A push channel can be set to work even when your browser is not active. For example, you could set it to show you a sport score if it changes. Push channels often use up a lot of *bandwidth**, which slows down your Internet connection.

Games

The Internet makes it possible to play *computer games** with people all over the world. Some games can be found on *Web sites**. These games often use *plug-ins**, and they allow you to play games with other users.

Other games can be played using commercial games services which work in a similar way to *ISPs**. You pay a fee depending on how much time you spend playing. With these services, you either have to buy the game on *CD-ROM**, or you may be able to download it from the Net.

A racing game which can be played on the Internet

Board games, such as Monopoly, can be played against people anywhere in the world.

You can play Pool and other sports against other people.

Bandwidth, 19; Browser, 30; CD-ROM, 43; Computer games, 42; Downloading, 19; E-mail, 28; File, 25; Internet/Net, 28; ISP, 28; Net, 28; Online, 18; Plug-in, 31; Program, 44; Virtual Reality, 42; Virtual world, 42; Web site, 30; Window, 26

🌐 Other uses

The *Internet** or *Net** is proving to be a very versatile tool for businesses and personal users. Shopping and banking *online**, without unauthorized users getting access to personal information, has been made possible by **secure *servers****. These are servers which *encrypt** sensitive information, such as credit card numbers, sent from a computer. This means that orders for goods can be placed securely.

It is also possible to *download** computerized money, or **e-cash**, onto your computer, to use it in banks and exchange it with suppliers for goods. Buying and selling goods and services using the Internet is sometimes called **e-commerce**.

Online forms make it possible to send information using the *Web**. An online form is part of a *Web page** where you can type in information which is then sent over the Net. This is how *search engines** work. It also makes it possible to take part in petitions or voting online, and send **feedback** to a site to say what you think of it.

An online form for ordering books

🗣 New developments

The Internet has rapidly developed from a specialist military and scientific *network** to a worldwide network used by

💻 Safety

Many people are concerned about how safe the Internet is for children and young people. Because it is so large, and is not **regulated** or controlled, some Web pages and chat rooms (see facing page) are not suitable for children.

There are a number of ways to make using the Web safer. Many sites now have **ratings**. These recommend who the site is suitable for. Some *browsers** can be set to block access to sites with certain ratings. The system is organized by **RSACi** (the **Recreational Software Advisory Council on the Internet**).

RSACi's Web site gives an explanation of how their rating system works.

Another way to block access to unsuitable sites is by using a **Web filter**. This is a *program** which monitors Web sites which are being visited, and blocks access to unsuitable ones. It can also be set to screen *e-mail** messages. **Net Nanny** and **SurfWatch** are both examples of Web filters.

The SurfWatch Web site

Net Nanny's Web site tells you how to get hold of the program.

millions of people. It will continue to develop and change very quickly in the future.

WebTV is a system which is designed to add the *interactive** elements of the Web to television. For example, a Web TV programme about cookery might enable you to get more information about recipes, or to order specific ingredients online.

The way information is transmitted is also likely to change in the future. Most people currently use a *modem**

to connect to the Internet. It is possible that *satellite** signals could be used instead. These, along with Web TV signals, would need to be received by a **set-top box** next to your computer, and a **satellite dish** attached to your house.

A company called **Norweb** has demonstrated that data can be sent along **high voltage power lines**. It may prove to be possible to deliver the Internet using these power lines, which already exist in most countries.

Design software

Design *software** is used for designing all sorts of things, from books, buildings and aeroplanes to transport routes, machines and maps. It provides a **computer simulation**, or imitation, of real life, allowing you to create all kinds of layouts and drawings.

*This map was created using GIS** *(Geographical Information Systems), a kind of design software for making maps.*

 ## Design tools

When you use design software, you draw and **manipulate** (change around) your designs using a range of different *functions** called **tools**. You choose a tool by selecting an *icon** from a group of icons known as a **toolbox** or **palette**. With a **customizable toolbox** or **palette**, you can choose the tools you want and arrange them to suit your own needs.

Lines called **guides** and **rulers** can be laid out to help you position your design correctly. A fixed arrangement of guides and rulers is called a **template**. For example, if you were designing a book, you would probably use the same template for each page.

The design you are creating might be much bigger than the screen on your *monitor**. To help you see the whole design, you can **view** (look at) the design at different sizes, **zoom** (look at part of the design in close-up), and *scroll** or **pan** (move around the design to look at different parts of it).

 ## DTP

DTP (**DeskTop Publishing**) is a *computerized** way of designing the layout of *text** and pictures in publications, such as books, magazines and leaflets. DTP software lets you create, move and change text and pictures in all sorts of ways. You can write text onto the screen, but cannot create pictures. These have to be imported (see below).

• **Page** An imitation on the screen of an actual page. Designers often work on two facing pages (called a **spread**) at one time.

• **Text box** or **frame** A frame around a piece of text. You can move and rearrange the text by moving the text box.

• **Import** To bring other data, such as a *graphic**, from another *file** or *application** and put, or **place**, it on your page.

• **Resize** To change the size of a picture or text box. You can also **rotate** (spin), **skew** (twist), **crop** (trim) and **stretch** pictures and text boxes.

• **Text wrapping** or **wrapping** Arranging text in a shape that fits neatly around a picture.

• **Tracking** or **kerning** Changing the space between *characters**, to make them more squashed together (called **tight tracking**) or more spaced apart (called **loose tracking**).

• **Edit tool** You choose this when you want to write text onto the page or make changes to the text already there.

• **Drawing tools** These are used to draw rectangles, circles, lines (called **rules**) and ovals on the page. A **line function** lets you choose the thickness of the lines or outlines and a **fill function** lets you fill in shapes with colour or a pattern.

*A spread from a book being designed with a DTP program**

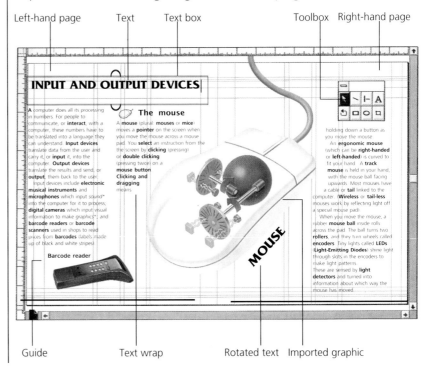

Left-hand page Text Text box Toolbox Right-hand page

Guide Text wrap Rotated text Imported graphic

CAD

CAD (Computer-Aided Design) *software** is used by designers to draw 3-D designs of buildings, vehicles, furniture and all sorts of other things.

The first stage is to make a **wire frame** or **wire mesh design**, which is made up of a network of thin lines.

Wire frame design for a jet plane

Then the wire frame design is **rendered**, or made solid-looking. The spaces can be filled in with colour, or with patterns called **hatching**. Some CAD software uses a technique called **ray tracing** to make the object look as if a light is shining on it from one side. The imaginary space the design is in is called the **model space**.

CAD software makes it easy to draw, or **define**, shapes using special *functions**. **Filleting** and **trimming functions** automatically make your drawing neater and more accurate. You can choose perfect circles and rectangles from a selection of pre-defined shapes called **primitives**. An **aerial view function** lets you see the whole of your design in one corner of the screen, while you look at one part in close-up.

Rendered design

Solid-looking surface

The object is made to look as if light is shining on it.

For complicated designs, a method called **hiding** can be used. Different levels, or **layers**, of an object can be built up on top of each other. One layer could show the outside of a building, while the layer beneath showed the water pipes and electricity wires inside.

CAD software design for a part of an engine

CAD software design for a building

Testing

CAT (Computer-Aided Testing) software is used to test CAD designs (see above). You can use it to **visualize**, or see, a design behaving like a real object. There are several types of testing including **resistance testing**, which imitates the flow of air or water around an object, and **crash testing**, which can simulate a vehicle in a crash.

One testing method is called **finite element analysis**. A design, such as a car windscreen, is divided into small pieces called **elements**, and each element is given **material properties** - descriptions of the weight and qualities of different substances, such as glass. Then you can **model**, or imitate, a real situation. For example, you could see where and how the wind-screen would break in a crash.

*Virtual Reality** can be used to let testers "walk around" inside a design for a large structure, such as a museum or a railway station, before anything is built. This helps prevent possible problems such as congestion.

Part of a Virtual Reality design for a garage. You could "go into" this design and explore the garage as if it were real.

Function, 4; Software, 4, 24; Virtual Reality, 42

Graphics software

Graphics *software** can be used to create pictures, or to change and *process** pictures that you put into a computer. **Computer graphics** means any kind of picture made or processed by a computer.

Computer graphics are sometimes called **Computer-Generated Imagery (CGI)**. Processing graphics is called **image processing** or **Digital Image Processing (DIP)**.

Any picture displayed by a computer is made up of rectangular *pixels** - tiny dots on the screen of your *monitor**. Graphics can be divided into two categories: **bitmapped graphics**, where each pixel is controlled individually, and **vector graphics**, where each pixel is controlled using a mathematical formula worked out by the computer.

Bitmapped pictures use a large number of pixels, usually set out in a grid pattern. The pixels become more visible the more the picture is magnified.

A bitmapped picture with a section enlarged

Vector graphics can be magnified without losing the quality of the image, because the mathematical formula creating the image does not change.

The size of a picture is measured by how many pixels there are in its height or width. This is called *resolution**. A monitor displays a grid pattern of pixels, called **monitor resolution**. Monitors are often set up to display 800 pixels across and 600 pixels high. Pictures which use a lot of pixels are *high resolution**. Pictures on a screen often look fuzzy or jagged, because the screen or picture is *low resolution**: it does not use enough pixels to show the image clearly. This jaggedness is called **aliasing**.

Graphics software has many creative uses, such as making computer art, cartoons, and special effects for films. Graphics are also used in *games**, *CAD** and other software.

Analysis graphics are used to represent information in a visual way to make it easier to understand - for example, by turning information in the form of numbers into pictures, called **graphs** or **charts**.

Presentation graphics are used to make visual information more interesting, for example by making it 3-D or more colourful.

A pie chart created using analysis graphics

The same pie chart enhanced using presentation graphics

 Hardware

You sometimes need special *hardware** to use certain kinds of graphics software.

A **graphics card** or **video card** is an *expansion card** which allows graphics to be displayed on your computer. If you want to have good **video graphics**, or moving pictures, you need a lot of *memory** and *processing power**. Some graphics cards contain a kind of *RAM** called **VRAM (Video Random-Access Memory)**. This helps video graphics work faster.

You might also use a **mouse pen**. This looks like, and is held like, a pen or pencil, but it has a small ball at the tip, like a mouse, and is attached to the computer by a *cable**, or by an *infra-red transmitter**.

A *graphics tablet** or **graphics pad** is also available. You draw on this with a special pen, or **stylus**, and your drawing appears on the screen. A stylus is easier to draw with than a mouse.

A **digitizing tablet** is a very sensitive type of graphics tablet used for *animation**, *retouching** and CAD software. It is used with a very accurate *mouse** called a **digitizer mouse**. This has a **sight** that sticks out at the front. It marks the mouse's position very precisely.

Digitizer mouse

Sight

*Animation, 38; Cable, 17; CAD, 35; Expansion card, 8; Games, 42; Graphics tablet, 16; Hardware; 4; Infra-red transmitter, 17; Memory, 22; Monitor, 7; Mouse, 7; Pixel, 7; Processing, 4; Processing power, 9; RAM, 22; Resolution, High/Low, 7; Retouching, 38; Software, 4, 24

Paint packages

A **paint package** is a piece of *software** which lets you create your own graphics. Using a *graphics tablet** or a *mouse**, you can draw and paint in different styles, known as **brushes. Roller, airbrush** and **eraser** are examples of styles. You can choose different brush widths, and more advanced paint packages have many variations to each brush. For example, you can set the brush to draw a thick or thin line depending on how hard you press with a stylus (see facing page). This is called a **pressure-sensitive brush** or **pressure-sensitive stylus**. Some brushes can create repeating designs. For instance, each time you make a mark on the paper, an identical flower could appear.

You choose colours, styles and so on from a **paint palette**, a kind of *toolbox**, sometimes called a *toolbar**, on the screen.

Pictures created using paint packages

Paint packages are often used to create complicated images for advertising.

Each toolbox has a number of **toggle buttons**. These are the buttons you *click** on to activate the brush you want to use.

Some packages allow you to replace a colour in your picture with another one. This is called a **fill command**. It is also possible to *cut and paste** a small piece of your picture, to add it to another area.

Many packages have **user-definable brushes** and **palettes**. This means you can design your own styles (called **customized styles**) and keep them for whenever you need them.

Paint effects

Paint effects packages let you change pictures that already exist. For example, you can *scan** a picture into the computer and then make it look like an oil painting or a drawing, or like a blurred photograph. The different effects are called **filters**.

These pictures have been processed using graphics filters.

Computer art

Graphics software is used to create amazing works of **computer art**, or **digital art**. Some are done with paint packages, and others use mathematical formulae, such as **fractals** (short for **fractional dimension**) and **sets**, to build up complicated patterns. Graphics software is also used to create **random-dot stereograms**. These appear to be abstract patterns, but if you look at them in a certain way you can see a 3-D image. Fractal art is used in advertisements and television programmes.

Computer art created using a fractal formula

A 3-D model created on a computer

More graphics software

Compositing

Compositing or **image compositing** means putting together parts of different pictures to make them look like one new picture. You can also do this with moving pictures (**video compositing**). For example, you can composite two photographs to make it look as if two people have had their photograph taken together, even if they have never met. You can also **delete**, or **edit out** (remove), parts of pictures and fill in the space with something else. This is called **retouching**, or **touching up**. For example, you can *scan** in a photograph of a person, and retouch it to alter their features.

You can also change parts of pictures to make them a different size or shape. This is called *resizing**, or **rescaling**.

There are a variety of techniques to reduce the *aliasing**, or jaggedness, of images when compositing, or **editing**, them. Some *paint packages** allow you to blur the edges of an image, or shade along the edge to make its transition from dark to light less

The top two pictures have been composited to create the third.

distinct. Using one of these methods to remove the aliasing is called **anti-aliasing**.

For instance, using compositing methods you could create a photograph of a person hanging off a cliff. The person's photograph is taken from a safe place. The cliff photo can then be added using compositing methods.

Animation

Animation means making moving pictures. **Computer animation** means using *graphics software** to make or edit animated pictures. Animation *applications**, or **digital cartooning systems**, let you create images and make them move. **Multilayered 2-D animations** show flat characters in front of flat backgrounds. **3-D animations** show three-dimensional characters and backgrounds.

Animations are made up of a series of still pictures put together in sequence to look like moving pictures. Each still picture is called a **frame** or **cel**. To see the pictures running together smoothly in a sequence, the animation must run at a speed of 24 **frames per second** (**fps**). This means that 24 still pictures are flashed in sequence in one second. Computers can be used to do most of the complex work involved in creating each frame. This is called **rendering**. For a long sequence of frames, a computer can take a few days to finish rendering.

Some computer animation techniques are described here.
• **Polygon modelling** Creating a **model**, or 3-D shape, out of polygons. A polygon can be a shape with straight edges, a circle, text, lines, or other shapes. **Spline-based modelling** means making the model out of curved shapes.
• **Lofting** Making a model by allowing a shape to follow a determined path. For example, lofting a circle polygon shape along a straight line path will create a pipe-shaped model.
• **Data capture** or **grabbing** Filming or photographing real objects to use as models, instead of creating models on screen. The model has specific points (such as the joints on a human) marked with sensors, so that a computer can take a 3-D capture of the movement. **Motion capture** is similar, but the model's movement is recorded on a film which picks up the sensors. Both techniques are sometimes used in computer games where realistic movements are needed.
• **Photogrammetry** and **rotoscoping** Ways of filming an object from lots of different angles. Each photograph is pieced together by the computer to create a 3-D model made up of all the pieces. Once a model is made, it can have a skin, or **texture map**, applied to give it colour, or a special surface. For example, a model of a door could have a texture map of a picture of a door applied, to make it look more realistic.
• **Inbetweening** or **tweening** To do this, the animator marks points, called **keys**, on two shapes. The computer fills in all the stages in between, so that it looks as if one shape has been turned into another.

Inbetweening (see facing page)

The key points are marked on each image. The computer fills in the stages in between to create the appearance of movement.

 ## Graphics files

There are many different *file extensions** for graphics *files**. Some programs can use several different types of file. The most common types of file for still, or **static**, images are **.gif** (**Graphics Interchange Format**), **.jpg** (**JPEG**, short for **Joint Photographic Experts Group**), **.tif** (**TIFF**, short for **Tagged Image File Format**), and **.bmp** (**bitmap**). Moving images, or video clips, often use **.avi** (**Audio Video Interleave**) or **.mov** (*QuickTime** **movie**). **Animated gifs** are moving images which are created using several images. The images are played in sequence to create an animated image. They are often used on the *World Wide Web**, as they are quick to *download**, and can be used to create new moving *cursors**. These can be used to make your computer's display more interesting.

 ## Special effects

Graphics software* is used to make many kinds of special effects for films. **Morphing** means changing one film image into another, using inbetweening (see facing page). This is commonly used to change an image of one person into another.

Blue screen effects are used to provide different backgrounds. For instance, by filming someone in front of a blue backdrop, filmmakers can later remove it and replace it with a new background using a computer.

This animated monster was created for a science fiction film using graphics software.

A **flocking algorithm** is a *program** that can help animate a number of objects at once, such as a crowd of people. This means that a scene can involve a huge crowd of people, many of whom can be *computer-generated**.

Masking is used when an area of the frame (see facing page) needs to be hidden. This is normally when something is going to be composited into the picture later. You can also distort parts of a person or object, and mix animated characters with real actors in the same film.

Sound and music software

Sound *software** is software for *processing** sounds. Some sound software can recognize the human voice, and imitate speech. Other software is used to mix musical sounds, or create completely new sounds. Processing sounds on a computer is called **audio processing** or **Digital Audio Processing (DAP)**. **Computer-generated sound** is sound created using a computer.

Any sound that you can hear exists in the form of **sound waves** which travel through the air to your ears. These waves are a kind of *analog** signal. Computers can only work using a *digital** signal (a signal made up of *bits** instead of waves). A device called an **Analog-Digital (AD) converter** converts sound waves into digital signals so they can be processed, and a **Digital-Analog (DA) converter** turns them back into sound waves.

Sound cards

If you want to use sound software on a *personal computer**, you usually need to add a **sound card**, a type of *expansion card**. Sound cards are usually either 16-bit or 32-bit. **16-bit sound cards** can give **CD-quality sound** (sound that is as realistic as a music *CD**). **32-bit sound cards** give even higher quality sound. Some sound cards have a **synthesizer** *chip** which **synthesizes**, or imitates, real sounds. Others have a **wave table**, a store of recordings of sounds. These are called **samples**.

Mixing music

Most modern music is composed and then put together, or **mixed**, using computers. The main method of recording music is called **digital recording**. Another method is by recording instructions, or musical input, into a *computer system** called a **MIDI (Musical Instrument Digital Interface) system**. This gives the computer instructions, such as how long to play a sound for, instead of digitally recording the actual sound. The recordings are then changed or **edited**, using a control desk called a **mixing desk**. Unwanted noises can be removed using a **digital noise reduction system** or **noise gate**. The recordings can then be arranged, or **sequenced**, and joined, or **spliced**, together to make the final result.

MIDI recording software lets you mix music on a *Mac** or *PC**, if you have a sound card. You can see the music in written form, and edit it using all the features of a mixing desk.

MIDI recording software

Talking

Voice recognition software can analyze and recognize human speech. It usually works by **word recognition** - that is, recognizing the sounds of individual words when they are spoken separately. Word recognition software converts each word into a pattern, and then compares the patterns with each other to work out which word is which. This method is called **pattern-matching**.

Word recognition software is usually used in **voice-controlled** *word processors**, **dictation software** or **voice-input systems**. You speak into a microphone and your words appear written on the screen. You can use specially *programmed** **voice commands** to give other instructions, so you don't have to use your hands at all. This is ideal for people who have *RSI** or other injuries or disabilities.

Voice recognition software usually has to "learn" to recognize a particular voice before it can work properly. It does this by building up a **voice file**, a record of a person's **acoustic models** (patterns representing speech). It then compares the words it "hears" to these models.

Speech synthesis software is software that imitates human speech. One type, called a **text-to-voice system**, can turn written words into spoken words which the user can hear. This is useful for blind people and for people who can write, but can't speak very clearly.

The screen in this picture shows the pattern made by the word "baby".

A woman using DragonDictate voice recognition software

♪♫ Instruments

Electronic or **digital musical instruments**, such as **electronic keyboards** and **electronic pianos**, are *computerized** instruments. They store computer-generated recordings (see facing page) in the form of *digital** code. This is converted into sounds you can hear by a Digital-Analog converter (see facing page) in the instrument.

Some computerized instruments, like the **electronic drum kit** in the picture, are played normally. Others, such as a **drum machine** or a **synthesizer** (a machine which imitates real sounds) can be *programmed** to create different digital sounds and play them in different sequences. A **sampler** is used

Electronic music synthesizer

Liquid Crystal Display

Volume control

YAMAHA W7

Keyboard

These controls let you "bend" or distort sounds.

These buttons let you create different kinds of sound.

Control unit

Drum pad

Stand

Foot pedal for bass drum

Electronic drum kit

to record and play back samples (see facing page).

Sounds stored using MIDI systems (see facing page) can be bought in collections called **banks**. These can be *installed** on a computer, and controlled from almost any kind of musical instrument.

♪♫ Music styles

Several different styles of music are made using sound *software**. **Ambient music** is gentle, atmospheric music, often made by mixing samples (see facing page) of sounds from nature. It often has special

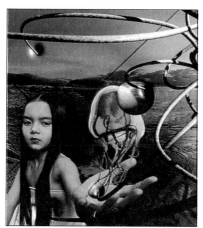

Ambient music graphics, or "visuals"

computer *graphics** called **visuals** to go with it. Computer-generated rhythms are used to create many styles of music, including **techno**, **drum'n'bass**, **house** and **jungle**.

Electro-acoustic music is serious electronic music (not pop) that brings together computer and traditional music. In France, a centre called **IRCAM** (**Institut de Recherche et de Coordination Acoustique/ Musique**) explores ways in which computers can create musical sounds, especially for live or **real-time performances**. Pierre Boulez is a famous electro-acoustic composer.

Sound software is also used to make weird music and **sound effects** (special or unusual sounds) for *games** and films. This is done using

sound software *programs** called **effects algorithms**.

♪♫ Music storage

Music takes up a lot of storage space in a *computer system**, and does not always fit on *floppy disks**. It can be stored on *optical discs**, *zip disks**, *jaz disks**, *rewritable discs**, or on **Digital Audio Tape** (**DAT**), a kind of cassette tape.

Music that is sold in the shops can be stored in a digital form on *compact discs** or on a kind of disc called a **MiniDisc** (**MD**).

SONY MD

MiniDisc player

*Compact disc, 23; Computerized, 4; Computer system, 4; Digital, 4, 19; Floppy disk, 23; Games, 42; Graphics, 36; Installing, 25; Jaz disk, 23; Optical disc, 23; Program(ming), 44; Rewritable disc, 23; Software, 4, 24; Zip disk, 23

41

Games, entertainment and education

Computers can be used for fun, and for learning and training. **Computer games software*** is one of the most popular of all types of software. Some games, especially those for children, are designed to be educational as well. Multimedia software (see facing page) is often both entertaining and educational, and is sometimes called **infotainment** or **edutainment software**.

 Games

There are many different types of computer games, also called **video games**. You can play an **arcade game**, a large, *dedicated*** game-playing machine, in an amusement arcade, or a tiny **hand-held** or **pocket computer game** which can be carried anywhere. A **Tamagotchi** is a tiny computerized pet or **cyberpet**. **Games computers** or **games consoles** are games machines which you plug into a television. You can also play a wide range of games on a *personal computer***. Some games can be played against other players on the *Internet***.

A Tamagotchi

People who play computer games are called **gamers**. A computer game's action, or **gameplay**, is represented by *graphics*** and *sound***. **Video-quality graphics** are high-quality graphics that look.like film. With **real-time graphics**, the action is realistic and runs at the same speed as real life. A **sprite** is an animated character on the screen. Games are usually played using a *joystick***.

Here are some of the many types of games software.

• **Combat**, **hack'n'slash** or **action game** A fighting game.

Screen showing a combat game

• **Adventure game** A game in which you explore a territory, such as a castle, jungle or alien planet. **Role-playing** and **fantasy games** are similar.

• **Space combat** or **space war games** Fighting games involving battles in space.

• **Simulation games** These recreate the experience of flying a plane (**flight simulation**), or driving a vehicle. In **racing games**, you race against other vehicles or planes.

• **Topographical games** These let you control an imaginary city or civilization, using various methods of government.

• **Strategy games** Strategy games let you play one side in a battle or conflict. You are given plenty of time to plan your moves carefully.

• **Sports games** There are lots of these, such as computer golf, soccer and baseball.

 Virtual Reality

Virtual Reality (**VR**) means using 3-D graphics to create an imaginary world, or **virtual world**, which surrounds the user. **Desktop VR** appears on a PC *screen***. You can use VR to play games or explore imaginary places.

You need special **VR gear** (equipment) to use VR. A **VR headset** or **head-mounted display** shows graphics on a screen in front of your eyes. As you turn your head, the picture on the screen moves around too, so it feels as if you are in a 3-D world. A **dataglove** or **VR glove** is a glove with **pressure pads** which make your hand feel as if it is picking up objects or touching surfaces. You use a kind of *mouse***, called a **VR mouse**, **3-D mouse** or **virtual mouse**, to move around in **virtual space** - the imaginary space you are exploring.

A Virtual Reality user wearing VR gear

Screen in front of eyes, showing 3-D picture

Headset

Dataglove

3-D mouse

Cables

👁️🦻 Multimedia

Multimedia means using computers to combine *text**, *sound**, *graphics** and video. **Multimedia *software**** usually comes on a **CD-ROM (Compact Disc Read-Only Memory)**, a kind of *compact disc**. It can also come on **DVD (digital video disc** or **digital versatile disc)**, a type of CD-ROM which can hold more information.

Multimedia software includes games, information CD-ROMs (or **electronic books**), and other types of educational software. Most CD-ROMs are **interactive** - you take part in what happens and choose the things you want to see and hear, using a *mouse**. For example, in a multimedia CD-ROM about nature, you might look up the word "parrot" and choose from a photograph of a parrot, a **digital video clip** (a short piece of moving film), a sound recording of a parrot squawking, some text to read, and a map showing where parrots live.

To use multimedia, you need a set of extra *hardware** called a **multimedia bundle** or **kit**. This includes a **CD-ROM *drive**** for playing CD-ROMs, **speakers**

A multimedia-ready computer

Microphone lets you record your own sounds.

Left speaker

Right speaker (two speakers give realistic sound effects)

Screen

Headphones let you listen to sounds.

CD-ROM drive for playing CD-ROMs

Joystick

or **headphones** so you can hear the sounds, and a *sound card** and a *graphics card**. Most *personal computers** are sold **multimedia-ready** or **multimedia-prepared** - already fitted with multimedia equipment.

Some multimedia software uses a system called **hypertext**. In hypertext, some words, called **hypertext words**, are highlighted. If you *click** on a hypertext word, the screen shows more information about that subject. **Hypermedia** is similar, but works with pictures as well as text. Some software can connect up to the *Internet**.

A screen from a CD-ROM

🎓 Learning

Computer software can help • people learn in all sorts of ways. Educational CD-ROMs (see above) invite the user to select answers or objects from a choice on the screen, using the mouse. This is called **interactive learning**, **collaborative learning**, or **point-and-click learning**. Multimedia software is also useful for learning subjects that involve sound, such as music and languages.

Simulation training means using computer graphics or Virtual Reality (see facing page) to train pilots, doctors and other workers. The computer simulates (imitates) the situation they will have to work in, so they can practise and make mistakes without causing any harm.

This machine for training pilots simulates an aeroplane's cockpit.

Programming

A computer program is a set of instructions which a computer uses to do a particular task. Computer programs are pieces of *software**. Writing computer programs is called **programming**. Although computers seem very clever, a computer can't do anything unless somebody writes a program to tell it how. Computer programs are written in programming languages (see right). The words and symbols used to write a program are called **code**. The way a program solves problems is called **program logic**.

Program makers

Most programs are written by specially trained **computer programmers**. Many of these work for **software houses** or **software publishers**, companies that produce *software packages**. Others work for companies called **computer consultancies**, which write software to order, according to their customers' own requirements. As well as programmers, companies like these have **software engineers** and **software designers** who decide what kind of software is needed and how it will work.

Large companies often have an **applications development department** which produces software just for their company. They have *systems analysts** to find out what software is needed, and programmers to write it.

Creating new software is called **software development**. Some programmers, such as *applications** **programmers** and *systems** **programmers**, specialize in writing certain types of software.

⟨100110⟩ Languages

Computers use a language called *binary code** or **machine code**. Writing programs in machine code is very difficult and slow, so a **programming language** is used to write the program in a code called the **source code** or the **source program**. Other programs then translate this into machine code.

High-level programming languages are made up of words, just like real languages, and are the easier type to use. They are translated by either an interpreter program or a compiler program. An **interpreter program** translates the source code line by line as the program is *running**. A **compiler program** translates the whole program into chunks of a simpler code, called the **object code**. A program called a **linker** then links the chunks together to make an *executable** - a program the computer can run.

Low-level programming languages are made up of numbers and symbols. They are translated by programs called **assemblers**.

Programming language levels

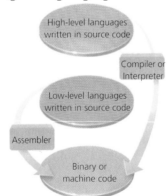

Several programming languages are listed on the right. They are all high-level

languages. Some are **problem-oriented languages** - languages designed for a particular purpose.

• **BASIC (Beginner's All-purpose Symbolic Instruction Code)** An easy language which is used to teach programming.

• **Visual Basic (VB)** is a language often used to write *Windows** applications.

• **Logo** This simple language was invented by a scientist called Professor Seymour Papert, to help children learn about programming. Logo instructions control the movements of a *computerized** *robot** turtle, which draws pictures by moving around the floor holding a pen.

Seymour Papert's turtle

Picture

• **FORTRAN (FORmula TRANslation)** A language often used to write mathematical and scientific software.

• **COBOL (COmmon Business Oriented Language)** Made for writing business programs, such as payroll (wages) software.

• **Pascal** A language used by computer scientists, and often taught to computer students.

• **C** and **C++** Advanced languages, widely used for general programming.

• **Ada** An advanced language designed for military uses.

• **PROLOG (PROgramming in LOGic)** A very advanced language used mainly for *artificial intelligence** software.

• **4GL (Fourth Generation Language)** A name for programming languages that resemble human language.

• **Java** A language used to write programs called *applets**, commonly used for *Web pages**.

**Applet, Applications, 24; Artificial intelligence, 52; Binary code, 20; Computerized, 4; Executable, 25; Robot, 15; Running, 24; Software, 4, 24; Software package, 25; Systems (software), 24; Systems analyst, 14; Web page, 30; Windows, 26*

Writing programs

There are usually three main stages in writing a program: designing, coding and testing.

Designing the program involves deciding what the program should do and how it should work. The programmer draws a diagram called a **flowchart** showing the different stages of the program. (A **macro flowchart** is rougher and more general.) The program may then be written out in **pseudocode**, or normal words.

Next, the programmer writes, or **codes**, the program in source code (see facing page), using **software tools** - programs which help write code. These include an **editor** or **text editor** (a kind of *word processing** program) and a **debug tool** or **debugger**, which helps find **bugs**, or mistakes. There are lots of ways to code one program. Coding a program well is called elegant programming.

When the program is written, the programmer *runs** it to see if it works. This is called **alpha testing**. The program is also tested by a sample of users called **beta testers**. Any bugs are corrected, and the programmer makes **tweaks** (small changes). This is called **debugging** or **bug fixing**.

Maintenance

Even when a program has been published (sold to the public), it can still have bugs (see left). **Program maintenance** means checking and improving a piece of *software** throughout its **life cycle** (the period of time when it is in public use). The programmer writes a detailed description of how the program works, called **program documentation**. This helps other programmers to **reprogram** or **reconfigure** (rewrite) parts of the code. The company that produced the software usually also has a **user support service**. Users can telephone or *e-mail** the service if they need help, and can report any bugs they find.

When a program has been improved, it is often released as a new **version**. Many programs go through dozens of different versions during their life cycles.

Software versions

Program words

• **Program decomposition** Splitting a programming job into sections called **modules** or **segments**, which can be written by different programmers.
• **Algorithm** or **routine** A piece of code which does a particular job. Programmers keep a selection of algorithms, called an **algorithm library** or **program library**, to use instead of writing new code.
• SQA (**Software Quality Assurance**) Making sure a program is ready to be published, using **software metrics** - methods of measuring how well a program works and giving it a score.
• SLOC (**Source Lines Of Code**) The number of lines of source code (see facing page) a programmer writes per day or month. Used to measure a programmer's speed.
• **Loop** Part of a program that is repeated several times.
• **Nest** A piece of code inside another piece of the same type, such as a loop within a loop.
• **Top-down programming** A name for the most common method, or **approach**, for writing programs.

A flowchart, pseudocode and source code for a simple password program.*

Flowchart

- Start
- Print message
- Get user input
- Check password
- If password is right
- Print "OK"
- End

- If password is wrong
- Print "Error"

Pseudocode

```
WHILE password
not OK

  PRINT "Enter
  today's password"

  GET input from
  user

  IF password OK
  PRINT "OK"

  ELSE PRINT "Error"
  END IF

END
```

Source code (the program) written in C (see facing page)

```
#define PASSWORD "robot"

main ( ) {
  int password_ok = 0;
  char input [80] ;

  while (!password _ok) {

    printf ("\nEnter today's
    password: \n") ;

    gets (input) ;

    if (strcmp (input,
    PASSWORD) == 0) {
      printf ("Password
      accepted. \n") ;
      password_ok = 1;
    }
    else printf ("%s is not
    today's password!\n",
    input) ;
  }
}
```

Computer problems and solutions

Computer systems* are complicated and can go wrong. For example, *hardware** can be faulty and *software** can have *bugs**. Computers are also at risk from crime, such as hacking, virus-writing and pirating. Using computers could even damage your health.

Systems failure

Computer failure is often called **systems failure** or **crashing**. A computer that is not working is said to be **down** or **crashed**. A **hang-up** means your computer does not respond when you try to use the *mouse** or *keyboard**. The amount of time that a computer system is not working is known as the **equipment downtime**.

When computers fail, you can often lose the data you are working on. This is why you need to *back up** (keep copies of) all your data. Many types of software have *functions** such as **autobackup** and **autosave**, which automatically keep copies of your data as you work.

Here are some different kinds of computer problems and some possible solutions.

• **Static interference** Damage caused to data by static electricity (a form of electricity which builds up in objects). An **anti-static** or **earthed mouse mat** can help to stop this.

Earthed mouse mat

Earthing cable carries static electricity away.

Mat

Mouse

• **Buggy chip** A *chip** that has something wrong with it. The problem can sometimes be cured using a program called a **software patch** or **Service Pack** to replace the incorrect instructions in the chip.
• **Hard disk fragmentation** happens when the data on your *hard disk** gets disorganized. It can be tidied up by **defragging** - using a **defragmentation program** to sort out the data.
• **Corrupt disk** A damaged disk (either hard or *floppy**) that doesn't work properly.
• **Screen burn** or **burn-in** used to happen on *screens**. An image that was left on screen for a long time could become imprinted on the glass. *Programs** called **screen savers** were developed, to replace the image with a moving picture after a certain amount of time. Today they are still used, but only to decorate the screen.

A screen saver

Computer crime

There are several kinds of **computer crime**. **Computer theft** is common, because computers are very valuable. A **chip heist** is a burglary where chips are stolen from inside computers. **Computer fraud** means changing data in a computer, for example to cover up crimes such as embezzlement (stealing money from a company you work for). **Spoofing** means trying to sabotage (damage) data by deliberately making a computer system go wrong.

Measures to prevent theft and fraud are called **computer security**. A **case lock** locks the *case** of your computer. A **disk drive lock** locks your *disk drive** so no one else can use it. A **removable hard disk*** can be taken out of your computer and locked away to keep data safe.

Disk drive lock

Software piracy means copying (or **pirating**) a piece of software to use or sell. To prevent pirating, some software companies supply a **dongle**, a plug which fits into the back of the computer. The software will only work when its dongle is in place, so pirated copies are no use.

Dongle

Hacking

A **hacker** is a person who tries to **hack into** or **break into** (gain entry to) computers, to look at, change or destroy data. This is usually done by **cracking** (finding) the *password** that protects the data on a computer. Hackers are sometimes called **electronic outlaws** or **electronic terrorists**.

Data can be **encrypted** (written in code) so that hackers can't make sense of it, and then **decrypted** (decoded) when it is needed. **Data protection** means trying to keep data safe from hackers and other criminals.

*Backing up, 23; Bug, 45; Case, 12; Chip, 21; Computer system, 4; Disk drive, 23; Floppy disk, 23; Function, 4; Hard disk, 23; Hardware, 4; Keyboard, 6; Mouse, 7; Password, 18; Program, 36; Screen, 7; Software, 4, 24

Viruses

A **computer virus** is a *program** which can attach itself to other programs and reproduce itself, spreading from one computer to another through a *network** or on *floppy disks**. Viruses are written deliberately by criminals called **virus-writers** to damage *data**, or just to annoy people.

Viruses can make strange things happen to your data, or write messages on your screen.

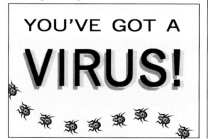

YOU'VE GOT A
VIRUS!

Some viruses (**joke viruses**) are harmless, but some can destroy all your data. Some, such as the **Queeg virus**, leave a rude message on the screen. Famous viruses include the **Michelangelo virus** and the **Jerusalem virus**, which all destroy, or **trash**, data, and the **Cascade virus**, which makes the *characters** on the screen fall into a heap at the bottom.

Here are some types of virus:
- **Macro virus** A virus which is *encoded** as a *macro** in a *document**. Once the document is opened, the virus is replicated each time a new document is created in the same program.
- **Trojan horse** or **Trojan** A virus that gets into a computer by disguising itself as another, safer, program.
- **Worm** A virus which can

reproduce itself independently, without having to attach itself to other programs.
- **Logic bomb** A virus which is activated when a particular program is *running**. A **time bomb** is a virus that only affects a computer on a certain date.
- **Intended virus** A virus that doesn't work as it was meant to.

A computer that is affected, or **infected**, by a virus is called a **host**. **Anti-virus programs** (or **vaccines**) and **virus checking programs** can ensure that your computer detects, or **diagnoses**, viruses.

*Some anti-virus programs, such as **Norton Anti-Virus**, show graphics** on the screen when they detect a virus.*

⚠ User safety

Using a computer for a long period of time can be bad for you. Sitting in a bad position can give you backache or neck ache, and light reflecting off the screen (called *glare**) could hurt your eyes.

Injuries to the wrists and hands can be caused by using the *keyboard** and *mouse**. These include **Repetitive Strain Injury** or **RSI**, often caused by typing, and

tendinitis, **tenosynovitis** and **carpal tunnel syndrome**, which are inflammations of the tendons leading to your fingers.

To avoid injury, you should take a regular 10-minute break, or **screen break**, every hour, shake your hands and wrists and

look around the room. Safety equipment such as **wrist rests** and **foot rests** can help you sit in a safe position, and an *ergonomic** or **hand-shaped mouse** and **ergonomic keyboard** can help reduce strain.

Ergonomic keyboard

The unusual shape of this keyboard makes it very comfortable to use.

Mouse mat with a built-in wrist rest

Your wrist rests on here.

Hand-shaped mouse

Your fingers fit in these grooves.

Scan of a hand affected by carpal tunnel syndrome. Blue and pink show inflamed, painful areas.

Foot rest

You can change the angle of the foot rest.

Your feet rest flat on this non-slip surface.

Character, 6; Data, 4; Document, 25; Encoding, 7; Ergonomic mouse, 7; Floppy disk, 23; Glare, 7; Graphics, 36; Keyboard, 6; Macro, 56; Mouse, 7; Network, 18; Program, 44; Running, 24

Living with computers

The number of computers in the world is rising very rapidly. In the last twenty years, computers have changed the way we do all sorts of everyday things, such as shopping, working and finding out information. These changes are often referred to as the **computer revolution**, the **digital revolution**, or the **information technology revolution**. People who have grown up with computers are often called the **digital generation**.

The word "**cyber**", which comes from the Greek word *kubernan* meaning "to control", often appears in computer words. For example, **cyber-culture** means computer culture, a **cyber-society** means a *computerized** society, and **cyberskills** are computer skills.

If you understand computers, you are **computer literate** or **computerate**. **Cyberphobia** is a fear of computers, and **technophobia** means fear of anything technological. These fears can sometimes stop people using computers, and are known as the **FUD (Fear, Uncertainty and Doubt) factor**.

In many parts of the world, people do not have access to computers, usually because they are poor. Even in developed countries such as the UK, not everyone has the same access. If you have access to computers and information, you are **information rich**; if not, you are **information poor**.

 Information

Computer technology is often called **Information Technology (IT)** because computers have had such a big effect on the way information is stored and spread.

The media (such as television, newspapers and magazines) is one of the main areas to be affected. **Online media** or **paperless media** means using a computer *network** to spread information. For example, **online newspapers** can be sent straight to your screen instead of being printed on paper. **TV on demand** or **video on demand systems** let you choose a film or programme to watch, which is then sent to your television over a network. Videos can also be stored on *CDs** called **video CDs**, and played on a **video CD player** linked to your television.

Museums often use computers to make exhibits more exciting. **Animatronics** means using computers to control *robots**. It is used to make moving exhibits showing animals or machines.

Information once stored in books can now be kept in a **virtual library** or **electronic library**, stored on *CD-ROMs**. Writers have also used CD-ROMs for *hypertext** **novels**. You can read some parts of a hypertext novel in any order, so the story can develop in different ways.

Living in the **information age** today means having access to a huge amount of information. You can select from a vast array of information, which may not all be relevant, and which could be confusing. Having too much information to choose from is called **information overload**.

Schools

Computers are frequently used in schools and colleges. Many schools are connected to the *Internet** so that they can work on projects with other schools around the world. Computers are used by students to produce work or find out information, and by staff to keep records, including *databases** of attendance, and timetables. They can also be used to assist in teaching.

Computers are often used in schools.

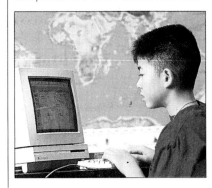

An animatronic dinosaur from a museum exhibition

*CD, 23; CD-ROM, 43; Computerized, 4; Database, 27; Hypertext, 43; Internet, 28; Network, 18; Robot, 15

Jobs

Many people now work from home, using computer *networks** to link themselves to their workplace. This is called **telecommuting** or **tele-working**. A **telecottage** or **telecentre** is a local centre where people share the use of computers, *fax** machines and other equipment which helps them telecommute.

This woman is telecommuting using a notebook* computer.

The digital revolution (see facing page) has also created lots of new jobs. As well as computer *programmers** and engineers, companies need people called **IT** (see facing page) **trainers** or **IT instructors** to teach their employees how to use computers. To create products such as *CD-ROMs**, specially skilled **multimedia* authors** and **multimedia designers** are needed. You might find a job like this in **online postings** - job advertisements which you can find on the *Internet**.

Computers have replaced people in some jobs. For example, computerized banking has led to a decrease of nearly a fifth of the bank workforce, as calculations can be done by computer. Other jobs can be done by workers abroad, as *data** can be transferred on a network.

 ## Shopping

Computers are being used to make choosing and paying for shopping easier. Computerized *EFTPOS** systems let you pay for goods using **payment cards**, such as **direct debit cards**, which transfer money straight from your bank account. Another kind of card is a **smart card**.

A smart card cut-away to show the chip* inside

Computer-processed photo of card holder

A chip inside the card stores information.

The card is thicker than a normal payment card.

A smart card can store units of value and other information. You can "**charge up**" your card by paying to have units put on it, and then use it to pay for things. Some shops use smart cards called **loyalty cards**, which store information about what you have bought and how much you have spent. The shop's computer can read this data from the card and give you discounts. This is called a **loyalty scheme**.

Many shops use a *computerized* barcode scanner** to read the price of an item. Computers in the shop can keep track of what items are in stock, and can instantly re-order items which are selling out. Some shops have **self-scanning**. You scan the things yourself, and an extra scanner spots anything you miss out.

A system called a **tagging system** can even read the price of everything in a trolley or basket without you having to take the things out, by tagging the items with labels called **passive radiant tags**.

Some shops have **in-store touchscreens*** and **multimedia* systems** to give you information - for example, to show you a map of the store or print out a recipe.

Home shopping, also called **virtual shopping** or **online shopping**, is another way to buy goods, using a television or a computer connected to a network. You choose from a range of items on the screen. With some clothes shopping systems, you can see the clothes *composited** onto a photo of yourself, to see how they would look. This is called a **virtual mirror**. Catalogues of goods, or **virtual catalogues**, can be sent to you on *CD**.

A kind of computer called an **HHCT (Hand-Held Computer Terminal)** can be used in shops and restaurants. For example, a waiter might take your order, type it into his HHCT, and transmit it instantly to a computer *printer** in the kitchen.

Display

A Hand - Held Computer Terminal (HHCT)

Barcode scanner, 6; CD, 23; CD-ROM, 43; Chip, 21; Compositing, 38; Computerized, 4; Data, 4; EFTPOS, 15; Fax, 19; Internet, 28; Multimedia, 43; Network, 18; Notebook, 13; Printer, 10; Programmer, 44; Touchscreen, 15

49

Living with computers

 ## Clever inventions

Computers are being used to help disabled people in various ways. A **videophone** uses a computer *network** to link two screens together, so that deaf people can see each other using sign language on the telephone. This is called **computer-telephony** or **video-telephony**.

A **functional electronic stimulus system** is being developed which can help paralysed people walk. The system stimulates the muscles with electrical signals, so they can make walking movements.

A man using a computerized stimulus system to help him walk

Computerized control unit attached to waist

Wires carry electrical signals to legs.

Walking frame for extra stability

In the home

There are probably lots of computers in your home which you are not aware of. For example, washing machines, video recorders and some alarm clocks contain computers.

Lots of people use *PCs** for work, to play games, or to connect to the *Internet**. A *games console** is a computer which is designed for games, and normally does not have a *keyboard**. The **Sony PlayStation** and **Sega Genesis** are both games consoles.

A Sony PlayStation

Many people use computers to *word-process** letters, communicate using *e-mail**, or find out information on the *World Wide Web**.

Some parents worry that their children will use computers too much, and suffer from **computer addiction**. This could mean using the computer instead of talking to friends or doing other things. Some people do spend longer than they should in front of a *screen**, but it is common to use computers with friends, and to learn new skills.

Many people use **time management *software***, which works as a computerized alternative to a diary or calendar. At home or in the workplace, you can use it to remind yourself of an appointment, or a bill you need to pay on a certain day.

Home banking has been made possible by computers. Many banks let you contact them by telephone or using the Internet. You can then organize your money automatically, without visiting the bank.

As the Internet expands, many people who do not own a PC can access it using public facilities. These include **cybercafes**, cafes where you can pay to use the Internet. Many libraries also have computers which you can use to access the Net.

Digital broadcasting

Terrestrial broadcasting services (television and radio signals, including those transmitted by *cable** or *satellite**) have previously been transmitted using *analog** signals. Now ***digital*** **broadcasting** has been introduced to improve television and radio services. When digital signals are used instead, more channels can be transmitted, and there is no *interference** to the picture or sound. Digital broadcasting also enables broadcasters to transmit **widescreen** pictures, of the kind you would see at the cinema. They can also include *interactive** features, enabling viewers to take part in programmes or find out more information on the screen.

A widescreen television

The history of computers

A computer really means a machine that helps you to do calculations. Simple counting machines, such as the **abacus**, have existed for thousands of years. However, the development of complicated modern computers, like the ones in this book, did not really begin until the nineteenth century. This time chart shows the most important dates.

An abacus is made from moving beads arranged on rods.

1833-4 The mathematician Charles *Babbage** started work on his **Analytical Engine**, the forerunner of the modern computer. It was mechanical and used punched cards, cogs and wheels instead of electronic signals. Babbage was helped by another mathematician called **Ada Augusta, Countess Lovelace**.

Ada Lovelace

Charles Babbage's Analytical Engine, which was only completed after his death

1930-40 Punched card computers were widely used for doing large calculations. They all used **decimal code**, the counting system which uses the digits 0-9.
1937 A British mathematician called **Alan Turing** invented a theoretical design for a computer, known as the **Turing machine**. This was used during the later development of computers.
1941 A German scientist, **Konrad Zuse**, built the first computer to use *binary**.
1945 The first completely electronic computer, **ENIAC** (**Electronic Numeric Integrator And Calculator**), was built by **Presper Eckert** and **John Mauchly** for the US Army.
1947 The *transistor** was invented. Early transistors were bigger than modern ones, and got very hot.
1948 The **Manchester University Mark I**, the first computer able to store *programs**, was completed.

An early transistor

1951 The **Ferranti Mark I**; an improved version of the Manchester University Mark I, went on sale.
1960 The first silicon *chips** were produced. This made it possible to build much smaller computers.
1964 The first computers built using silicon chips went on sale.

Silicon chip

1975 The first small home computer, the **Altair**, was sold. The *software** company **Microsoft** was founded in the USA by **Bill Gates** and **Paul Allen**.
1976 A new computer company, Apple Computer, was founded in the USA by **Steve Jobs** and **Steve Wozniak**. **Apple 1**, Apple's first computer, was built and went on sale.

1980 The **Sharp PC 1211**, the first *portable**, was launched.

Sharp PC 1211

1981 IBM (International Business Machines) introduced the *IBM PC**, a model that set the standard in small computers for the next few years. Microsoft brought out *MS-DOS**, an operating system *(OS*)* for use with IBM PCs.
1982 The electronics company *Intel** produced its 286 chip.
1983 Microsoft introduced the *Microsoft Windows** operating system.
1984 Apple introduced the Apple Macintosh (*Mac**), a computer built to rival the IBM PC.
1985 Intel released its 386 chip.
1986 Author **William Gibson** invented the word *cyberspace** in his novel *Neuromancer*.
1991 Apple, IBM and a company called Motorola announced a partnership to develop the **Power PC chip**. IBM and Apple computers could use the same software.

William Gibson

1993 Intel introduced the *Pentium processor™** chip.
1994 Apple and IBM launched the *Power Mac** and *Power PC**.
1995 Microsoft launched the *Windows 95** operating system.
1996 Intel introduced the *Pentium II** chip. Digital broadcasting (see facing page) launched in France.
1998 Microsoft launched the *Windows 98** operating system.
1999 Microsoft launched the **Windows 2000** operating system to replace *Windows NT**.

The future

A lthough computers have revolutionized the world, there are lots more changes to come. Nobody knows exactly what will happen as computers become more powerful. Some amazing inventions are being developed. Others are just ideas.

Communication

Lots more people will join the *Internet**, making communication much easier. The phrases **global village** and **digital community** describe a world where everyone is linked together by computers. Using the Internet, everyone will be able to find information easily.

Information will travel much faster than it does now. A new *network** called *ISDN (Integrated Services Digital Network)** has started to replace telephone wires with **digital telephone lines**, which carry data in a *digital** form using a very high *bandwidth**. A device called a *terminal adaptor** is used instead of a *modem**.

Soon, you will also be able to buy a **telecomputer**, or **teleputer**, a machine which is a television, a computer and a telephone all in one.

Intelligence

Scientists are researching ways to make computers think like human beings. This is called **AI** or **Artificial Intelligence**. AI scientists often use specially designed *programming languages**, such as **Lisp**.

Neural networks or **neural nets** are computers or *programs** that are designed to work like the human brain. **Fuzzy logic** means a computer can recognize a range, or **fuzzy set**, of different levels of certainty. Instead of understanding only "true" and "false", the computer can make value judgements, more like a person does.

Using a combination of AI and advanced engineering techniques, scientists may eventually create truly lifelike **androids** - *robots** that look and behave like humans. There are already some androids, but they are not completely realistic.

This android, called "Manny", was built by the US government for testing safety clothing.

The android can *simulate** sweating and breathing.

The android's movements can be very precise. They are controlled by a computer.

Hydraulic (fluid-pressured) engine systems make parts of the android move.

Manny is "fully articulated", which means his joints can move just like a person's.

Electrical signals are sent around the android's "body" along wires.

Virtual life

Virtual Reality* (VR) is already being used in lots of ways - for example, in medicine, entertainment and design. But VR is not yet very realistic. As techniques improve, though, VR could seem so real that

A scientist using Virtual Reality to "explore" a simulation* of the human brain

you could live a **virtual life** - having most of your experiences through VR. **Virtual travel systems** could take you on a **virtual holiday**, letting you experience other parts of the world through a *VR headset**. Even further into the future, people might one day be able to travel digitally, or **teleport**,

from place to place, instead of having to move around physically.

Some people even think that VR headsets might be replaced by a **DNI (Direct Neural Interface)** that would plug straight into your brain, and stimulate your brain cells to give you a **virtual experience**. A **brain implant** would work in a similar way, but would give you special skills, like being able to speak a new language or play an instrument, without you having to learn it.

*Bandwidth, 19; Digital, 4, 19; Internet, 28; ISDN, 19; Modem, 19; Network, 18; Program, 44; Programming language, 44; Robot, 15; Simulation, 34; Terminal adaptor, 19; Virtual Reality, 42; VR headset, 42

Millennium bug

The **millennium *bug*** is a problem which many computers will face in the year 2000. Most early *programming languages** recognize dates using only two digits for the year, so 1972 would be 72. Lots of *hardware** and *software** has continued to use the same settings. This means that on January 1, 2000, many computers could malfunction, because their date setting will be reset to 1900. Some experts have predicted disastrous consequences, as computers on aircraft, or in hospital equipment, could fail to work properly. Governments and businesses are spending huge amounts of money to ensure that their hardware and software is checked, to make sure that it is **millennium-compliant**.

New gadgets

New technology frequently combines functions which previously required several different machines. For example, it is possible to buy mobile telephones which can send *faxes** or *e-mails**, and connect to the *World Wide Web**.

Energy control systems will become increasingly common in homes and offices. These are systems which regulate the use of electricity. They automatically switch off machines which are not being used, and can also regulate heating and lighting to ensure that energy is being used efficiently. If a building uses **solar panels**, an energy control system can regulate the position of the panels, to ensure they are facing the sun.

The **Global Positioning System**, or **GPS**, is a new development in navigation and travel. The system enables you to work out your exact position in the world. It was devised by the US military to keep track of personnel and equipment, but can also be used in cars to help find the best route. A tiny **receiver** containing a computer can be placed in a vehicle. This calculates its exact position, based on radio signals transmitted from *satellites**.

Early computers filled up whole rooms, but today a computer can be extremely small. This makes a number of new developments possible.

Wearables are tiny computers that fit into items of clothing. A display in an eyepiece can be used while you are walking about or doing other things. This can give you instant access to information. For example, wearables could switch the heating down in your room if you were too hot, monitor your heart rate and blood pressure if you were exercising, or enable someone at home to look at items in a shop you are visiting.

The eyepiece can display up-to-date information.

Batteries and extra equipment can be stored on other parts of the outfit.

Security

Property tagging can be used to make property more secure. *Chips** storing the owner's address, and any other information, can be **embedded** in (attached to) items such as electrical equipment, or even clothes. This makes it easier to recover stolen items, as their whereabouts can be traced electronically.

Internet problems

Many users find the *Internet** works very slowly. As more people use it, *data** sent takes longer to travel, as only a certain amount can move around at a time. Until computer systems and connections improve, the situation will probably get worse, and lead to regular **brown-outs**, when the Internet *crashes**.

However, as computer technology, *modems** and faster types of connection develop, the Internet is likely to improve in speed. Today's problems will probably disappear within the next few years.

A camera embedded in the glove can record images.

This person is wearing an outfit equipped with wearable computers, which could be used by a reporter.

Glossary of computer slang

 ## Internet slang

There is a lot of **Net slang**, or slang words connected with the *Internet**. These are changing and growing in number all the time, but some of the most common ones are listed here.

Burning Extracting *data** from somewhere that is supposed to be secure.

Carting Buying a "shopping cart" full of items on the Net.

Drilling down Going through several *Web pages** to get to the one you want.

E-com Electronic commerce: buying, selling and advertising on the Net.

E-zine A magazine available over the Net in the form of electronic data.

Hanging/hung When nothing is happening while you are connected to the Internet.

Information superhighway Slang words for the Net.

Juicer Someone who is completely engrossed in *surfing the Net**.

Lurking Reading the messages of a *newsgroup** without sending any yourself. This is one way to find out about a group.

Moderator Someone who monitors *newsgroups** and *Web sites** to ensure users obey the rules of netiquette (see right).

Net cult A *newsgroup** or other group representing "cult" interests, such as witchcraft, magic or drugs.

Net evangelist Someone who tries to persuade other people to use the Internet.

Net surfing (*Surfing the Net**) Exploring the Internet.

Net traffic *Data** moving around on the Internet.

Net users People who use the Internet. There are many other words for this, including **netizens** or **net citizens**, and **netheads**.

Netiquette The rules of polite behaviour, which you should keep to when using the Internet.

Netzine A magazine about the Internet.

Newbie A new Internet user or a new member of a *newsgroup**.

Newbie baiting Searching for newbies who aren't sure what they're doing, and teasing them.

Noise Ongoing conversation or chat in a *newsgroup**, especially conversation which is not very relevant to the topic of the newsgroup.

Shouting Writing messages in CAPITAL LETTERS to show you are in a bad mood.

Spamming Sending junk *e-mail**, especially when done deliberately to annoy someone.

Virtual mate A friendship or relationship that starts on the Internet. Meeting someone face to face whom you have first made contact with on the Internet is called **boinking**.

World Wide Wait Amount of time it can take to use the Net.

 ## Other slang

Computer-friendly Willing to use and learn about computers.

Computerholic Addicted to computers, or a person who is addicted to using their computer.

Core wars A game played by computer *programmers**, in which each player tries to write a *program** that will destroy the other player's program.

Eat up To use up a lot of *processing power** or *RAM**. Some *software** does this.

Front end This means the place where a user is when using a computer, especially when connected to a *network**.

Futz The styles that people use to decorate their *screens**.

Gulp A group of more than eight *bits** (so called because it is bigger than a *byte**).

Junking or **binning** *Deleting** something from a computer.

Liveware A computer slang word for people. Also called **wetware** or **the meat**.

Lunchbox A name for a *notebook** computer.

Mouse potato Someone who sits in front of a computer all day. This comes from "couch potato" - someone who watches television all day.

Nerd or **computer nerd** A rude word for someone who is obsessed with computers. A nerd can also be called a **geek**, a **dweeb**, an **anorak** or a **propeller head** (because in the US, computer nerds used to be depicted as wearing caps with propellers on top).

Nybble A group of less than eight *bits** (so called because it is smaller than a *byte**).

Phreaking *Hacking** into a computer via telephone lines.

Power-hungry Needing a lot of *processing power**.

Rodent A *mouse**.

Shutdown A computer fault or problem that stops a system from working.

Streaming *Downloading** *files** in chunks so that you can see/hear some of the file while the rest is loading.

Synthespian Computer-generated person.

Techie Someone who knows about the more technical aspects of computers.

Vapourware *Software** that exists only as a prototype or idea and has not been released.

Glossary of acronyms

This list provides a quick guide to some of the more common computer-related acronyms. The numbers show the page on which each acronym is explained. Some of the acronyms explained here do not appear anywhere else in the book.

AD Analog-Digital (converter) **40**
ALU Arithmetic Logic Unit **9**
BBS Bulletin Board System **19**
BIOS Basic Input/Output System **9**
bps bits per second **19**
CAD Computer-Aided Design **35**
CAM Computer-Aided Manufacturing **15**
CAT Computer-Aided Testing **35**
CAT Computerized Axial Tomography (scanner) **15**
CD Compact Disc **23**
CD-i Compact Disc-interactive **56**
CD-ROM Compact Disc-Read-Only Memory **43**
CGI Computer-Generated Imagery **36**
CISC Complex Instruction Set Computer (CPU) **21**
CMOS Complementary Metal Oxide Semiconductor (RAM) **22**
cps characters per second **11**
CPU Central Processing Unit **9**
CRT Cathode Ray Tube (monitor) **7**
DA Digital-Analog (converter) **40**
DAP Digital Audio Processing **40**
DAT Digital Audio Tape **41**
DBMS DataBase Management System **27**
DIP Digital Image Processing **36**
DNI Direct Neural Interface **52**
DOS Disk Operating System **24**
DP Data Processing (department) **14**
dpi dots per inch **11**
DRAM Dynamic RAM **22**
DTP DeskTop Publishing **34**
DVD Digital Video Disc/Digital Versatile Disc **43**
EFTPOS Electronic Funds Transfer at Point Of Sale **15**

EISA Extended Industry Standard Architecture (bus) **20**
ENIAC Electronic Numeric Integrator And Calculator **51**
EPROM Erasable Programmable ROM **22**
FAQ Frequently Asked Questions **29**
FLOPS FLoating point Operations Per Second **21**
FPS File Processing System **27**
Ftp File transfer protocol **29**
FUD Fear, Uncertainty and Doubt (factor) **48**
GB Gigabyte **22**
GUI Graphical User Interface **24**
HHCT Hand-Held Computer Terminal **49**
HTML HyperText Mark-Up Language **31**
IBM International Business Machines **51**
IC Integrated Circuit **21**
IP Internet Protocol **28**
IRCAM Institut de Recherche et de Coordination Acoustique/Musique **41**
ISA Industry Standard Architecture (bus) **20**
ISDN Integrated Services Digital Network **52**
IT Information Technology **48**
JANET Joint Academic NETwork. A *network** which connects universities and colleges in the UK, and forms part of the *Internet**.
LAN Local Area Network **18**
LCD Liquid Crystal Display **13**
LED Light-Emitting Diode **7**
MB Megabyte **22**
MCA Micro Channel Architecture (bus) **20**
MD MiniDisc **41**
MIDI Musical Instrument Digital Interface **40**
MIME Multi-purpose Internet Mail Extensions **28**
MIPS Millions of Instructions Per Second **21**
MPEG Motion Pictures Experts

Group (compression) **56**
MS-DOS Microsoft Disk Operating System **24**
NSFNET National Science Foundation NETwork **28**
OCR Optical Character Recognition (scanner) **16**
OS Operating System **24**
PAD Packet Assembler and Disassembler **19**
PC Personal Computer **4, 12**
PCB Printed Circuit Board **8**
PCI Peripheral Component Interconnect (local bus) **20**
PCMCIA Personal Computer Memory Cards International Association (expansion card) **20**
ppm pages per minute **11**
RAM Random-Access Memory **22**
RISC Reduced Instruction Set Computer (CPU) **21**
ROM Read-Only Memory **22**
RSI Repetitive Strain Injury **47**
SCSI Small Computer Systems Interface **23**
SIMMs Single In-line Memory Modules **22**
SLOC Source Lines Of Code **45**
SQA Software Quality Assurance **45**
SVGA Super Video Graphics Array **7**
TCP Transmission Control Protocol **28**
TLA Three-Letter Acronym
UI User Interface **24**
USB Universal Serial Bus **8**
VDU Visual Display Unit **7**
VESA Video Electronics Standard Association (local bus) **20**
VGA Video Graphics Array **7**
VR Virtual Reality **42**
WAIS Wide Area Information Service. A huge collection of information available to anyone using the *Internet**.
WAN Wide Area Network **18**
WP Word Processing **26**
WWW World Wide Web **30**
WYSIWYG What You See Is What You Get **26**

Glossary of extra words

This glossary contains some extra computer words you might come across which do not appear in the rest of the book.

Acoustic coupler A device used instead of a *modem** to connect a computer to a telephone line. It is attached to the telephone handset, so it can easily be used in public telephone boxes, and is useful away from the home or office.

Bells and whistles Noises that are part of a piece of *software**, or any special extras or gimmicks that are sold with computer equipment.

Bernoulli drive A very fast kind of *disk drive** which uses special flexible disks. The disks are held in the right place by the drive's spinning action.

Board Another name for an *expansion card**.

Boolean algebra A mathematical system which allows facts to be expressed as either "true" or "false" (the basis of computer language).

Broadband A cable or channel that can carry a large amount of data at once.

CD-i (Compact Disc-interactive) A kind of compact disc (*CD**), similar to a *CD-ROM**, but which works with a television instead of with a computer. CD-i discs need a special CD-i player which plugs into the TV. Like CD-ROMs, CD-i discs are used for both entertainment and education.

Colour thermal printer A colour *printer** that works by applying heat to specially coated paper.

Cyberguru A person who is famous in the world of computers, especially in relation to the *Internet**.

Daisy chain To link computers or other computer equipment together in series (in a chain) instead of in a ring or star shape, which is more common.

Data highway Another name for a *bus**. Buses are also known as **highways** and **trunks**, especially in the US.

Default An automatic setting often found in *software**. If you do not make a choice from a range of options, the computer will choose the default setting.

Digital rights or **electronic rights** Legal rights, such as copyright, relating to material that is created and stored using computer equipment.

Enhance or **computer-enhance** To improve something, especially pictures or sounds, using computers. For example, telescope pictures of outer space are often enhanced, or made easier to see, using **enhancement** *software**.

Geographical Information Systems (GIS) *Software** that is used to make and analyze maps and plans.

Glitch A *bug**, mistake or defect in a computer.

Invisible effects Using special *software** to remove unwanted bits from films. For example, you could film an actor "flying" on safety wires, and then remove the wires from the picture using a computer.

Keystroke The act of pressing one key on the *keyboard**.

Kilobaud A unit used to measure how fast data can travel along a cable or channel.

Logging Gaining access to a *network** or a computer, especially a *mainframe**, is called **logging in** or **logging on**. When you finish using the system, you **log out** or **log off**.

Macro A small *program**, or set of instructions. Many types of *software** allow the user to write macros to help save time. You can carry out, or **invoke**, a macro with just a couple of keystrokes (see left). Then it runs through all its instructions without any more keystrokes.

Mailbase A list of addresses for a particular special interest group on the *Internet**.

Mechatronics A combination of mechanics and electronics, often used in building computerized machines.

MPEG (Motion Pictures Experts Group) compression A method used to *compress** video data, so that it can be stored on *CDs**. There are two versions - **MPEG1** and **MPEG2**.

Multi-user games *Games** in which you can play against several other people, linked together on the *Internet**. Many of these are adventure games known as **Multi-User Dungeon (MUD) games**.

Natural language interface A *program** which lets the user give the computer instructions using natural language (the person's own natural way of expressing things) instead of specific words.

Near-zero footprint A phrase often used in advertisements to describe a piece of equipment that takes up hardly any space on a desk or table.

Object-Oriented Programming (OOP) A method of *programming**. The programmer writes several shorter programs, called **objects**. Instead of containing just instructions, each object can contain both instructions and data. The objects then work together to run the program.

*Bug, 45; Bus, 20; CD, 23; CD-ROM, 43; Compression, 23; Disk drive, 23; Expansion card, 8; Games, 42; Internet, 28; Keyboard, 6; Mainframe, 14; Modem, 19; Network, 18; Printer, 10; Program(ming), 44; Software, 4, 24

Online democracy A possible development in the future, which would allow people to take part in political debates, talk to the government, and even vote, using the *Internet**.

Online tutorial A lesson over the *Internet**, especially one that teaches someone how to use the Internet itself.

Parity A system which prevents data being corrupted (damaged) when it is being sent along electronic pathways inside a computer, or along cables to another piece of *hardware**.

Park When you move a computer, the *hard disk** can get scratched and damaged by its moving parts. To keep the disk safe, you park it using a *program** that prevents these parts from moving.

Personal information manager A piece of *software** that helps people organize their time and make lists of things to do and people to see. Also called a **contact manager**.

Phase diffusion or **spatial processing** Using a type of *software** to make 3-D music that surrounds an audience. It works by giving out sounds at fractionally different times from several different loudspeakers.

PKzip software or **PKware** A group of public domain (see below) *programs** used for *compressing** data.

Public domain *Software** that is available for anyone to use and that costs nothing. It is usually found on the *Internet**.

Robotic prosthetic A computer-controlled artificial limb or other artificial body part.

Router A computer that handles and redirects messages and other data that are being sent over a large *network**.

Simplex modem A type of *modem** that can only send data in one direction.

Soft A word used to describe computer equipment or processes that can be changed using *software**. For example, a **soft key** is a key that can have different purposes, depending on what software is being used. A **soft boot** means stopping and restarting your computer without switching it off.

Speaker-independent voice recognition A system that can understand anyone that speaks to it, just as a person can. This is still being developed.

Systems operator or **sysop** Someone who organizes and runs a service such as a Bulletin Board System (*BBS**).

TAN (**Total Area Network**) Any *network** that extends all over the world.

Tape streamer A *tape drive** which can be used to make a copy of everything on a computer's *hard disk**.

Telepresence A system which uses a *network** and specially designed *software** to make you feel as if you are somewhere you are not. This is used in **telesurgery** which allows surgeons to operate on someone who is a long way away from them. The surgeon sees a video of the patient, and uses special controls to send instructions to a very advanced *robot** which carries out the operation.

Telnet A facility on the *Internet** which lets you use another person's computer. Often used for playing multi-user games (see facing page).

Throughput The amount of work a computer or other piece of *hardware** can do in a given amount of time.

Touchtone phone A telephone which sends sound signals, or tones, when the buttons are pressed. The signals can be received by a computer. You can use a touchtone phone to order goods or book tickets (called **touchtone booking**) directly from a computer linked to the telephone system, without speaking to a real person.

Translation system *Software** that can translate a piece of writing from one language into another. This has not been fully developed, but it could eventually be used to help people communicate on the *Internet** and in other ways.

Transputer A type of computer which can process more than one piece of data at once. Transputers are not used very much because they are very difficult to write *programs** for. They are still being developed.

True colour monitor A *monitor** that can show the complete range of colours visible to people - over 16.4 million colours.

V42bis A standard type of *modem**. A V42bis modem can transmit 48,000 bits per second or *bps**. There are several other standard modem types. For example, **V32bis modems** and **Vfast modems** are slower than a V42bis.

Valves Parts which were used in computers before *transistors** were invented. Valves were larger and heavier than transistors, so computers had to be quite big too.

Wild card A symbol that can be used to stand for anything. The symbol ***** is often used as a wild card. For example, "**.txt*" means any *file** that ends with the *extension** ".txt".

*BBS, 19; bps, 19; Compression, 23; Extension, 25; File, 25; Hard disk, 23; Hardware, 4; Internet, 28; Modem, 19; Monitor, 7; Network, 18; Program, 44; Robot, 15; Software, 4, 24; Tape drive, 23; Transistor, 21

57

Index

Numbers

2-D animation, multilayered, **38**
3.5 inch floppy disk, **23**
3-D animation, **38**
3-D mouse, **42**
3-D user interface, **24**
4GL (Fourth Generation Language), **44**
5.25 inch floppy disk, **23**
8-bit bus, 20
16-bit bus, **20**
16-bit sound card, **40**
32-bit bus, **20**
32-bit sound card, **40**
64-bit bus, 12, **20**
286, 9, **12**, 51
386, 9, **12**, 20, 51
486, 9, **12**, 51
601, **12**
603, **12**
604, **12**
80486, Intel, **12**

A

@ ('at'), **28**
abacus, **51**
ac (in an e-mail address), **28**
acceptable use policy, **28**
access (to access a computer), **18**
access (to access parts of RAM), **22**
access, authorized, **29**
access time, **22**
accordion fold paper, **11**
acoustic coupler, **56**
acoustic model, **40**
acronyms, 55
action game, **42**
active link, **30**
AD (Analog-Digital) converter, **40**, 55
Ada, **44**
adaptor,
    graphics, **7**
    ISDN, **19**
    mains, **13**
    modem, **19**
    terminal, **19**, 28, 52
Adaptor, Peripheral Interface (PIA), **8**
addiction, computer, **50**
address (in RAM), **22**
address (on a LAN), **18**
address, e-mail, **28**, 30
address bus, **20**
Advanced Research Projects Agency
    NETwork (ARPANET), **28**
adventure game, **42**
aerial view function, **35**
AI (Artificial Intelligence), 44, **52**
airbrush, **37**
algorithm, **45**
    effects, **41**
    flocking, **39**
algorithm library, **45**
aliasing, **36**, 38
Allen, Paul, 51

alphanumeric key, **6**
alpha testing, **45**
alt (newsgroup topic), **29**
Altair, 12, **51**
ALU (Arithmetic Logic Unit), **9**, 55
ambient music, **41**
Analog-Digital (AD) converter, **40**, 55
analog signal, **19**, 40, 50
analysis graphics, **36**
analyst, systems, **14**, 44
Analytical Engine, 14, **51**
and gate, **21**
android, **52**
animated gif, **39**
animation, computer, 36, **38**
animatronics, **48**
anonymous ftp site, **29**
anorak, **54**
anti-aliasing, **38**
anti-glare filter, **7**
anti-static mouse mat, **46**
anti-virus program, **47**
Apple 1, **51**
Apple Computer, **12**, 51
Apple key, **6**
Apple Macintosh (Mac), 4, **12**, 51
applet, **31**, 44
application, **24**, 25, 26, 34, 38, 44
    core or basic, **26**
applications development
    department, **44**
applications programmer, **44**
applications section, **14**
applications software, **24**
approach (programming), **45**
arcade game, **42**
architecture, **4**, 9, 12, 21
arithmetic, fixed point, **21**
arithmetic, floating point, **21**
Arithmetic Logic Unit (ALU), **9**, 55
ARPANET (Advanced Research Projects
    Agency NETwork), **28**
array (in parallel processing), **14**
array (in RAM), **22**
art, computer, 17, **37**
art, digital, **37**
Artificial Intelligence (AI), 44, **52**
assembler, **44**
AT bus, **20**
AT (chip), **12**
'at' symbol, **28**
audio processing, **40**
Audio Video Interleave (avi), **39**
authorized access, **29**
autobackup, **46**
autofire button, **16**
auto resume, **13**
autosave, **46**
autosensing power supply, **13**
auto suspend, **13**
avatar, **32**
avi (Audio Video Interleave), **39**

B

Babbage, Charles, **14**, 51
BABT (British Approvals Board for

    Telecommunications), **19**
BABT-approved modem, **19**
Back button, **30**
back-up/backing up, **23**, 46
backwardly compatible, **20**
ballpoint mouse, **13**
bandwidth, **19**, 32, 52
bank, **41**
banking, 4, 50
barcode, **6**
barcode reader, **6**,
barcode scanner, **6**, 49
BASIC (Beginner's All-purpose Symbolic
    Instruction Code), **44**
    Visual (VB), **44**
basic applications, 26-27
Basic Input/Output System (BIOS), 8,
    9, 55
batteries, dual, **13**
battery,
    RAM, **22**
    Nickel Cadmium (NiCad), **13**
    Nickel Metal Hydryde (NiMH), **13**
battery pack, **13**
baud rate, **19**
BBC Computer, **12**
BBS (Bulletin Board System), **19**, 55, 57
Beginner's All-purpose Symbolic Instruction
    Code (BASIC), **44**
bells and whistles, **56**
Bernoulli drive, **56**
beta tester, **45**
bi-directional printing, **11**
binary code, 17, **20**, 44, 51
binary digit, **20**
binning, **54**
BIOS (Basic Input/Output System), 8, **9**, 55
bit, 17, 19, **20**, 21, 40, 54
bitmap (bmp), **39**
bitmapped graphics, **36**
bits per second (bps), **19**, 55, 57
black (in printing), **10**
    registration, **10**
black and white printer, **10**
block, **26**
blue screen, **39**
bmp (bitmap), **38**
board, **56**
boinking, **54**
bold text, **26**
bomb, logic, **47**
bomb, time, **47**
book, electronic, **43**
bookmark, **30**
Boolean algebra, **56**
booting up, **8**
Boulez, Pierre, 41
bouncing, **29**
box, text, **34**
bps (bits per second), **19**, 55, 57
brain implant, **52**
breaking into (a computer), **46**
brightness button, **7**
British Approvals Board for
    Telecommunications (BABT), **19**
broadband, **56**

Page numbers in bold type (eg 37) show where to find the main explanation of a word or phrase.

broadcasting,
    digital, **50**, 51
    terrestrial, **50**
brown-out, **53**
browser, 29, **30**, 31, 32, 33
browsing, **30**
brush, **37**
    airbrush, **37**
    eraser, **37**
    pressure-sensitive, **37**
    roller, **37**
    user-definable, **37**
bubblejet printer, **10**
bucket, **22**
    empty, **22**
    full, **22**
buffer, memory, **11**
bug, **45**, 46, 56
    millennium, **53**
bug fixing, **45**
buggy chip, **46**
built-in printer, **10**
Bulletin Board System (BBS), **19**, 55, 57
bundle, **16**
    multimedia, 16, **43**
bundled software, **25**
burn-in, **46**
burning, **54**
bus, 8, 12, **20**, 21, 55, 56
    16-bit, **20**
    32-bit, **20**
    64-bit, **20**
    address, **20**
    AT, **20**
    control, **20**
    data, **20**
    EISA, **20**
    expansion, **20**
    ISA, **20**, 55
    local, **20**
    MCA, **20**, 55
    multiplexed, **20**
    PCI, **20**, 55
    VESA, **20**, 55
    VL-bus, **20**
business, 4, 27, 44
business accounting software, **27**
business software, **27**
bus interface unit, **9**
bus LAN, **18**
busy, **4**
butler in a box, **17**
button,
    autofire, **16**
    Back, **30**
    brightness, **7**
    contrast, **7**
    degauss, **7**
    fire, **16**
    History, **30**
    monitor, 5
    mouse, 5, **7**
    navigation, **30**
    Refresh, **30**
    Reload, **30**
    reset, 5, **8**

    Stop, **30**
    toggle, **37**
byte, 17, **20**, 22, 54

C

C, **44**
C++, **44**
cable, 5, 6, 7, 10, **17**, 18, 19, 36, 50
    coaxial, **18**
    fibre optic, **18**
    keyboard, 5, 6
    mouse, 5, 7
    parallel, **17**
    printer, 5, **10**
    serial, **17**
cable modem, **28**
cache, 12, **22**
    disk, **23**
    Web page, **30**
cache memory, 12, **22**
CAD (Computer-Aided Design), 15,
    25, **35**, 36, 55
calculated cell, **27**
CAM (Computer-Aided
    Manufacturing), **15**, 55
camera,
    digital, 10, **17**
    digital video, 3, **17**
    Web, **17**
capacitor, **9**
capacitor (part of RAM), **22**
capacitor, RAM, **13**
capacity, **22**, 23
CAPS LOCK key, **6**
card, **8**
    direct debit, **49**
    expansion, **8**, 13, 19, 20, 22, 36, 40,
        56
    graphics, **36**, 43
    local bus expansion, **20**
    loyalty, **49**
    memory, **13**
    modem, **19**
    payment, **49**
    PCMCIA, **20**
    smart, 15, **49**
    sound, **40**, 43
    video, **36**
carpal tunnel syndrome, **47**
carry-and-park portable, **13**
carting, **54**
cartridge,
    data, **23**
    ink, **10**
    SyQuest, **23**
    tape, 14, **23**
    toner, **10**, 11
Cascade virus, **47**
case, 4, 8, **12**, 15, 46
    desktop, **12**
case lock, **46**
cashless payment systems, **15**
catalogue, virtual, **49**
CAT (Computer-Aided Testing), **35**, 55
CAT (Computerized Axial

    Tomography) scanner, **15**, 55
Cathode Ray Tube (CRT) monitor, **7**, 13, 55
CAT scan, **15**
CCD (Charge Coupled Device), **16**
CD (Compact Disc), **23**, 40, 41, 43, 48,
    49, 55, 56
    video, **48**
CD (Compact Disc) drive, 5, 43
CD-i (Compact Disc-interactive), 55, **56**
CD-quality sound, **40**
CD-ROM, 23, 25, 32, **43**, 48, 49, 55, 56
CD-ROM drive, 3, 8, **43**
cel, **38**
cell (in RAM), **22**
cell (in a spreadsheet), **27**
cell pointer, **27**
centralized computing, **14**
Central Processing Unit (CPU), 5, 8, **9**, 12,
    14, 20, 21, 55
    CISC, **21**, 55
    RISC, **21**, 55
    user-removable, **12**
centre controls, **7**
CGI (Computer-Generated Imagery),
    36, 55
character, **6**, 7, 10, 27, 29, 34, 47
character printer, **10**
character recognition program, **13**
characters per second (cps), **11**, 55
charge (electrical), **11**
Charge Coupled Device (CCD), **16**
charge up (a smart card), **49**
chart, **36**
chassis, **12**
chat room, **32**, 33
cheapernet, **18**
checkout, computerized, **15**
chip, 5, 8, 9, 12, 14, 15, 20, **21**, 22, 40,
    46, 49, 51, 53
    buggy, **46**
    CPU, 12, 14, 20
    Power PC, **12**, 51
    RAM, 8, 12, 20, 22
    ROM, 8, 22
    silicon, 3, **21**, 51
    synthesizer, **40**
chip heist, **46**
circuit, electrical, **8**, 21
CISC (Complex Instruction Set Computer)
    CPU, **21**, 55
clicking, **7**, 30, 31, 37, 43
clicking and dragging, **7**
client, **18**
client-server technology, **18**
clip-on trackball, 3, **13**
clock, 8, **9**, 21
clock cycle, **9**
clock cycles per second, **9**
clock doubling, **21**
clock rate, **9**
clock speed, **9**
clock speed indicator, 8, **9**
clone, IBM, **12**
closing (a file), **25**
CMOS (Complementary Metal Oxide
    Semiconductor) RAM, **22**, 55

---

*Page numbers in bold type (eg **37**) show where to find the main explanation of a word or phrase.*   **59**

infected, **47**
information age, **48**
information, digital, **20**
information manager, personal, **57**
information overload, **48**
information poor, **48**
information rich, **48**
information section, **14**
information superhighway, **54**
Information Technology (IT), **48**, 55
Information Technology (IT) department,
    14
information technology revolution, **48**
infotainment, **42**
infra-red transmitter, **17**, 36
ink cartridge, **10**
ink chamber, **10**
inkjet printer, 3, **10**, 11
input, **4**, 14, 15
    musical, **40**
    pen-based, **13**
input (as a verb), **6**
input and output devices, **6**, 8, 9, 13, 16
input device, **6**, 9, 13, 16
Input/Output port (I/O port), **8**
Input/Output System, Basic (BIOS), 8, **9**, 55
INSERT key, **6**
install, **25**, 41
Institut de Recherche et de Coordination
    Acoustique/Musique (IRCAM), **41**,
    55
in-store touchscreen, **49**
Integrated Circuit (IC), **21**, 55
Integrated Services Digital Network
    (ISDN), **19**, 28, 52, 55
integrated software, **25**
Intel, 9, **12**, 51
Intel 80486, **12**
Intel Inside®, **12**
Intelligence, Artificial (AI), 44, **52**
Intellipoint, 24
intended virus, **47**
interact, **6**
interactive, 33, **43**, 50
interactive, Compact Disc- (CD-i), 55, **56**
interactive learning, **43**
interface, **8**, 19
    3-D user, **24**
    modem, **19**
Interface, Direct Neural (DNI), **52**, 55
Interface, Graphical User (GUI), **24**, 55
interface, menu-driven user, **24**
interface, natural language, **56**
Interface, Small Computer Systems (SCSI),
    8, 55
Interface, User (UI), **24**
Interface Adaptor, Peripheral (PIA), **8**
interface unit, bus, **9**
interference, **17**, 18, 50
    static, **46**
internal modem, **19**
internal storage device, **23**
International Business Machines (IBM), 12,
    51, 55
Internet, 17, 18, 19, 25, **28**, 29, 30, 31,
    32, 33, 42, 43, 48, 49, 50, 52,
    53, 54, 55, 56, 57
Internet Access Provider (IAP), **28**

Internet facilities, **28**
Internet Protocol (IP), **28**, 55
Internet Relay Chat (IRC), **32**
Internet Service Provider (ISP), **28**, 29, 32
interpreter program, **44**
intranet, **18**
invisible effects, **56**
invoke, **56**
I/O port (Input/Output port), **8**
IP (Internet protocol), **28**, 55
IRC (Internet Relay Chat), **32**
IRCAM (Institut de Recherche et de
    Coordination Acoustique/
    Musique), **41**, 55
ISA (Industry Standard Architecture) bus,
    20, 55
ISDN (Integrated Services Digital
    Network), **19**, 28, 52, 55
ISDN (Integrated Services Digital
    Network) adaptor, **19**
ISP (Internet Service Provider), **28**, 29, 32
italic text, **26**
IT (Information Technology), **48**, 49, 55
IT (Information Technology)
    department, **14**
IT instructor, **49**
IT trainer, **49**

J

JANET (Joint Academic NETwork), **55**
jargon, computer, **3**
Java, 31, **44**
jaz disk, **23**, 41
jaz drive, **23**
Jerusalem virus, **47**
JK-type flip flop, **21**
job, **4**
Jobs, Steve, **51**
Joint Academic NETwork (JANET), **55**
Joint Photographic Experts Group (JPEG/
    jpg), **39**
joke virus, **47**
journey, virtual, **28**
joystick, 3, **16**, 42
JPEG (Joint Photographic Experts Group), **39**
jpg (Joint Photographic Experts Group), **39**
juicer, **54**
jukebox, medical, **27**
jungle, **41**
junking, **54**
justified text, **26**

K

K, **22**
KB (kilobyte), **22**
Kbyte, **22**
kerning, **34**
key, 4, **6**
    alphanumeric, **6**
    Apple, **6**
    CAPS LOCK, **6**
    CONTROL, **6**
    cursor control, **6**
    dedicated, **6**
    ENTER, **6**
    function, **6**

    INSERT, **6**
    PAGE DOWN, **6**
    PAGE UP, **6**
    RETURN, **6**
    SHIFT, **6**
    soft, **57**
    toggle, **6**
    Windows, **6**
key (animation), **38**
keyboard, 4, 5, **6**, 12, 13, 14, 24, 27, 29,
    46, 47, 50, 56
    ergonomic, 3, **47**
    touch-sensitive, **6**
keyboard, electronic (musical), **41**
keyboard cable, 5, 6
keyboard feet, **6**
keyboardist, **14**
keyboard port, **8**
keypad, 6, **27**
keystroke, **56**
keyword, **31**
kilobaud, **56**
kilobyte (KB), **22**
kit, **16**
    multimedia, 16, **43**

L

label, **27**
LAN (Local Area Network), **18**, 28, 55
    bus, **18**
    ethernet, **18**
    optical, **18**
    snowflake, **18**
    star, **18**
    token ring, **18**
land, **23**
language,
    problem-oriented, **44**
    programming, **44**, 52
Language, COmmon Business Oriented
    (COBOL), **44**
Language, Fourth Generation (4GL), **44**
Language, Page Description (PDL), **11**
laptop, **13**
laser beam, **11**, 23
laser printer, 10, **11**
layer, **35**
layout, page, **26**
LCD (Liquid Crystal Display), 7, **13**, 55
LCD monitor/screen, 7, **13**
lead (cable), **17**
learning, **43**
leased line, **19**, 28
LED (Light-Emitting Diode), **7**, 55
LED indicator, **8**
letter quality, **11**
library,
    algorithm, **45**
    data, **14**
    electronic, **48**
    program, **45**
    virtual, **48**
lid, detachable, **13**
life, virtual, **52**
life cycle, **45**
light detector, **7**

Light-Emitting Diode (LED), **7**, 55
line,
  data, **17**
  digital telephone, **52**
  leased, **19**, 28
line feed, 10, **11**
line function, **34**
line printer, **10**
lines, digital telephone, **52**
link,
  active, **30**
  followed, **30**
linked up, **18**
linker, **44**
Liquid Crystal Display (LCD), 7, **13**, 55
Lisp, **52**
list, mailing, **32**
listserv, **32**
literate, computer, **48**
live, **4**
"live" hypertext links, **30**
liveware, **54**
loading, **22**, 25
Local Area Network (LAN), **18**, 28, 55
local bus, **20**
  PCI (Peripheral Component
      Interconnect), **20**, 55
  VESA (Video Electronics Standard
      Association), **20**, 55
local bus expansion card, **20**
local change, **27**
local server, **19**
location, memory, **22**
lock,
  case, **46**
  disk drive, **46**
lofting, **38**
logging in, **56**
logging off, **56**
logging on, **56**
logging out, **56**
logic,
  fuzzy, **52**
  program, **44**
logic bomb, **47**
logic gate, **21**
logic-seeking print head, **11**
logic symbol, **21**
Logic Unit, Arithmetic (ALU), **9**, 55
Logo, **44**
long-distance mouse, **16**
loop (cable), **18**
loop (program), **45**
loose tracking, **34**
loudspeaker, **8**
Lovelace, Ada Augusta, Countess, **51**
low-level programming language, **44**
low-rad/low-radiation monitor, **7**
low resolution, **7**, 36
loyalty card, **49**
loyalty scheme, **49**
luggable, **13**
lunchbox, **54**
lurking, **54**

M

Mac (Apple Macintosh), 4, 9, **12**, 24, 40, 51

machine,
  drum, **41**
  facsimile/fax, **19**
  Turing, **51**
machine code, **44**
Macintosh, see Mac
Mac OS, **24**
Mac OS8, **24**
Mac, Power, **12**, 51
macro, 47, **56**
macro flowchart, **45**
macro virus, **47**
magenta (in printing), **10**
magnetic disk, **23**
magnetic strip, **15**
magneto-optical disc, **23**
mail, **19**
  e-, 19, **28**, 29, 30, 32
  electronic, **28**
  flame, **29**
  snail, **28**
mailbase, **56**
mailing list, **32**
mail-only connection, **28**
mainboard, **8**
mainframe, 4, **14**, 56
mains adaptor, **13**
maintenance, program, **45**
Management System, DataBase (DBMS),
    27, 55
manager,
  contact, **57**
  file, **25**
  personal information, **57**
Manchester University Mark I, **51**
manipulating, **34**
manual, **25**
margin, **26**
Mark I, Ferranti, **51**
Mark I, Manchester University, **51**
mark scanner, **16**
mask, **39**
mat, mouse, **5**
  anti-static, **46**
  earthed, **46**
  with wrist rest, 47
mat, scan, **16**
material properties, **35**
maths co-processor, **21**
matrix, **10**
matrix matching, **16**
Mauchly, John, **51**
maximize, **26**
MB (megabyte), **22**, 55
MByte, **22**
MCA (Micro Channel Architecture) bus,
    20, 55
MD (MiniDisc), **41**, 55
meat, the, **54**
mechatronics, **56**
media, 48
medical expert system, **27**
medical jukebox, **27**
meg, **22**
megabyte (MB), **22**, 23, 55
megaflop, **21**
megahertz (Mhz), **9**
memory, 4, 9, 11, 12, 13, 17, 20, **22**, 25, 36

cache, 12, **22**
Memory, Random-Access, see RAM
Memory, Read-Only, see ROM
memory buffer, **11**
memory card, **13**
memory location, **22**
Memory Modules, Single In-line (SIMMs),
    22, 55
menu, 24, 30, 31
  pull-down, **24**, 31
menu bar, **24**
menu-driven user interface, **24**
metaphor, desktop, **24**
Mhz (megahertz), **9**
mice, **7**
Michelangelo virus, **47**
micro, **12**
Micro Channel Architecture (MCA) bus,
    20, 55
microchip, **21**
microcomputer, **12**
microfloppy, **23**
microphone, 43
microprocessor, **9**
Microsoft®, 24, 51
Microsoft® Disk Operating System (MS-
    DOS®), 24, 51, 55
Microsoft® Internet Explorer, **30**
Microsoft® Outlook™, **29**
Microsoft® Windows®, 13, 24, **26**, 44, 51
Microsoft® Windows® 95, **24**, 25, 51
Microsoft® Windows® 98, **24**, 51
Microsoft® Windows® 2000, **51**
Microsoft® Windows® CE, **13**
Microsoft® Windows® NT, **24**, 51
MIDI-compatible, **41**
MIDI recording software, **40**
MIDI socket, **41**
MIDI (Musical Instrument Digital Interface)
    system, **40**, 41, 55
midi tower, **12**
millennium bug, **53**
millennium compliant, **53**
Millions of Instructions Per Second (MIPS),
    14, **21**, 55
MIMD (Multiple Instruction Multiple Data)
    parallel processing, **14**
MIME (Multi-purpose Internet Mail
    Extensions), 28, 55
minicomputer, **14**
MiniDisc (MD), **41**, 55
MiniDisc player, 3, **41**
minifloppy, **23**
minimize, **26**
mini tower, **12**
MIPS (Millions of Instructions Per Second),
    14, **21**, 55
mIRC, **32**
mirror, virtual, **49**
mixing, **40**
mixing desk, **40**
MMX™, **12**
model, **38**
model, acoustic, **39**
modelling, **35**
  polygon, **38**
  spline-based, **38**
model space, **35**

---

*Page numbers in bold type (eg **37**) show where to find the main explanation of a word or phrase.*

*Page numbers in bold type (eg **37**) show where to find the main explanation of a word or phrase.*

sprite, **42**
sprocket, **11**
SQA (Software Quality Assurance), **45**, 55
standalone computer, **18**
standard passive LCD screen, **13**
star LAN, **18**
start-up page, **30**
static electricity, 40
static images, **39**
static interference, **46**
static RAM, **22**
stationary, continuous, **11**
stereogram, random-dot, **37**
Stop button, **30**
storage device, 4, **22**, 23, 24
strain injury, see RSI
strategy game, **42**
streaming, **54**
stretching, **34**
strip, magnetic, **15**
style, customized, **37**
stylus, **36**, 37
      pressure-sensitive, **37**
sub-directory, **25**
subdomain, **28**
sub-notebook, **13**
subtopic, **29**
supercomputer, **14**
Super Video Graphics Array (SVGA), **7**, 55
support service, user, **45**
support staff, **14**
surfing the Net, **30**, 54
SurfWatch, **33**
suspend, auto, **13**
SVGA (Super Video Graphics Array), **7**, 47
switch, on/off, **8**
symbol, logic, **21**
synthesizer, **41**
synthesizer chip, **40**
synthesizing, **40**
synthespian, **54**
SyQuest cartridge, **23**
.sys (file extension), **25**
sysop, **57**
system,
      computer, **4**, 16, 40, 46
      operating, 22, **24**, 26, 51, 55
systems analyst, **14**, 44
systems failure, **46**
systems operator, **57**
systems programmer, **44**
systems software, **24**, 44
systems unit, **8**

T

tab, **26**
tablet,
      digitizing, **36**
      graphics, 3, **16**, 36, 37
tabulate, **26**
tag, **31**
      passive radiant, **49**
Tagged Image File Format (TIFF/tif), **39**
tagging, property, **53**
tagging system, **49**
tail, **7**
tail-less mouse, **7**
Tamagotchi, 3, **42**

TAN (Total Area Network), **57**
tape cartridge, 14, **23**
tape deck, **23**
tape drive, 5, **23**, 57
tape streamer, **57**
tape transport, **23**
task, **4**
TCP/IP (Transmission Control Protocol/
      Internet Protocol), **28**, 55
techie, **54**
technical support staff, **14**
Technical Word Processor (TWP), **26**
technician, **14**
techno, **41**
technobabble, **3**
technological warfare, **15**
technophobia, **48**
technospeak, **3**
telecentre, **49**
telecomms, **18**
telecommunications, **18**
telecommunications satellite, **18**
telecommuting, **49**
telecomputer, **52**
teleconferencing, **17**
telecottage, **49**
telephony,
      computer-, **50**
      video-, **50**
teleport, **52**
telepresence, **57**
teleputer, **52**
telesurgery, **57**
teleworking, **49**
Telnet, **57**
template, **34**
tendinitis, **47**
tenosynovitis, **47**
terminal, **14**
terminal adaptor, **19**, 28, 52
terminal connection, **28**
terrestrial broadcasting, **50**
terrorist, electronic, **46**
tester, beta, **45**
testing, alpha, **45**
Testing, Computer-Aided (CAT), **35**, 55
text, **5**, 6, 10, 16, 18, 24, 25, 26, 27, 31,
      34, 43
text box, **34**
text editor, 31, **45**
text file, **25**
text formatting, **26**
text frame, **34**
text-to-voice system, **40**
texture map, **38**
text wrapping, **34**
TFT (Thin Film Transistor), **13**
theft, computer, **46**
the meat, **54**
thick (coaxial cable), **18**
thicknet, **18**
thin (coaxial cable), **18**
Thin Film Transistor (TFT), **13**
thinnet, **18**
three-colour printing, **10**
Three-Letter Acronym (TLA), **55**
throughput, **57**
thumball, **13**
ticket, computer-coded, **15**

TIFF/tif (Tagged Image File Format), **39**
tight tracking, **34**
time bomb, **47**
time division multiplexing, **20**
time management software, **50**
timesharing, **14**
TLA (Three-Letter Acronym), **55**
toggle button, **37**
toggle key, **6**
token, **18**
token ring LAN, **18**
tone, continuous, **10**
toner, **10**, 11
toner cartridge, **10**, 11
tool, **34**
      drawing, **34**
      edit, **34**
      software, **45**
toolbar, **30**, 37
toolbox, **34**, 37
      customizable, **34**
top-down programming, **45**
topic, **29**
topographical game, **42**
topology, **18**
Total Area Network (TAN), **57**
touching up, **38**
touchpad, **7**, 13
touchscreen, **15**
      in-store, **49**
touch-sensitive keyboard, **6**
touchtone booking, **57**
touchtone phone, **57**
tower, **12**
track (electrical), **8**, 20
track (formatting), **23**
trackball, 3, **13**
trackerball, **13**
tracking (in DTP), **34**
      loose, **34**
      tight, **34**
tracking (with a hand scanner), **16**
track pad, **16**
trackpad, **7**
tractor, **11**
traffic, net, **54**
trainer, IT, **48**
transceiver, **18**
transistor, **21**, 51, 57
translation system, **57**
transmission, **17**
      duplex, **19**
      parallel, **17**
      serial, **17**
      USB, **17**
Transmission Control Protocol/Internet
      Protocol (TCP/IP), **28**, 55
transputer, **57**
trashing (data), **47**
travel system, virtual, **52**
trimming function, **35**
Trojan/Trojan horse virus, **47**
true colour monitor, **57**
trunk, **56**
Turing, Alan, **51**
Turing machine, **51**
TV on demand, **48**
tweak, **45**
tweening, **38**

TWP (Technical Word Processor), **26**
.txt (file extension), **25**
type, **26**
typeface, **26**
type size, **26**
typewriter, electronic, **15**

U

UI (User Interface), **24**, 55
underlined text, **26**
Uniform Resource Locator (URL), **30**
Universal Product Code (UPC), **15**
Universal Serial Bus (USB), **8**, 17, 55
UNIX, **24**
up and running, **4**
UPC (Universal Product Code), **15**
upgradability, **12**
upgradable, fully, **12**
upgrading, **12**
URL (Uniform Resource Locator), **30**
USB (Universal Serial Bus), **8**, 17, 55
USB port, **8**
USB transmission, **17**
Usenet, **29**
user, **4**
user-definable brush, **37**
user-definable palette, **37**
user-friendly, **4**
User Interface (UI), **24**, 55
username, **28**
user-removable CPU, **12**
user support service, **45**
user-unfriendly, **4**
utility software, **24**

V

V32bis modem, **57**
V42bis modem, **57**
vaccine, **47**
value, **27**
valve, **57**
vapourware, **54**
VB (Visual Basic), **44**
VDU (Visual Display Unit), **7**, 55
vector graphics, **36**
version, **45**
VESA (Video Electronics Standard
        Association) local bus, **20**, 55
Vfast modem, **57**
VGA (Video Graphics Array), **7**, 55
Vic 20, **12**
video camera, digital, 3, **17**
video card, **36**
video CD, **48**
video CD player, **48**
video clip, digital, **43**
video compositing, **38**
video conferencing, **17**
Video Electronics Standard Association
        (VESA) local bus, **20**, 55
video, freeze frame, **17**
video, full motion, **17**
video game, **42**
video graphics, **36**
Video Graphics Array (VGA), **7**, 55
video on demand, **48**
videophone, **50**

video-quality graphics, **42**
Video Random-Access Memory (VRAM), **36**
video-telephony, **50**
videotex system, **27**
view, **34**
virtual catalogue, **49**
virtual experience, **52**
virtual holiday, **52**
virtual journey, **28**
virtual library, **48**
virtual life, **52**
virtual mate, **54**
virtual mirror, **49**
virtual mouse, **42**
virtual RAM, **22**
Virtual Reality (VR), 32, 35, **42**, 43, 52, 55
virtual shopping, **49**
virtual space, **42**
virtual travel system, **52**
virtual world, 32, **42**
virus checking program, **47**
virus, computer, 46, **47**
virus-writer, **47**
Visa cash, **15**
vision systems, **15**
Visual Basic (VB), **44**
visual data, **27**
Visual Display Unit (VDU), **7**, 55
visualizing, **35**
visuals (for ambient music), **41**
VL-bus (VESA local bus), **20**
voice command, **40**
voice-controlled word processor, **40**
voice file, **40**
voice-input system, **40**
voice recognition software, **40**
volatile, **22**
VR (Virtual Reality), 32, 35, **42**, 43, 52, 55
        desktop, **42**
VRAM (Video Random-Access Memory), **36**
VR gear, **42**
VR glove, **42**
VR headset, **42**, 52
VR mouse, **42**

W

wafer, **21**
WAIS (Wide Area Information Service), **55**
WAN (Wide Area Network), **18**, 28, 55
warfare, technological, **15**
wave, sound, **40**
wave table, **40**
wearable, **53**
Web, the, **30**, 31, 33
Web browser, see browser
Web cam, **17**
Web camera, **17**
Web editor, **31**
Web filter, **33**
Web page, 29, **30**, 31, 33, 44, 54
        default page, **30**
        entry page, **30**
        home page (default), **30**
        home page (on a site), **30**
        start-up page, **30**
Web site, **30**, 31, 32, 54
WebTV, **33**
wetware, **54**

What You See Is What You Get
        (WYSIWYG), **26**, 31, 55
wheel, scrolling, **7**
Wide Area Information Service (WAIS), **55**
Wide Area Network (WAN), **18**, 28, 55
widescreen, **50**
wild card, **57**
WIMP (Windows, Icons, Mouse and
        Pointer) interface, **24**
window, **26**, 29, 30, 32
window, scanner, **16**
Windows®, see Microsoft® Windows®
Windows® 95, Microsoft®, **24**, 29, 51
Windows® 98, Microsoft®, **24**, 51
Windows® 2000, Microsoft®, **51**
Windows® CE, Microsoft®, **13**
Windows Explorer, **25**
Windows, Icons, Mouse and Pointer
        (WIMP) interface, **24**
Windows key, **6**
Windows® NT, Microsoft®, **24**, 51
wire, **17**
wire, data, **17**
wire frame design, **35**
wire mesh design, **35**
wired (on a network), **18**
wired (slang), **28**
wizziwig, see WYSIWYG
word, **21**
wordcount, **26**
Word Processing (WP), **26**, 45, 50, 55
word processor,
        dedicated, 10, **15**
        voice-controlled, **40**
word recognition, **40**
word wrap, **26**
workgroup, **19**
work-on-the-go portable, **13**
worksheet, **27**
workstation, **15**, 24
World Wide Wait, **54**
World Wide Web (WWW), 17, **30**, 31, 39,
        50, 53, 55
worm (virus), **47**
WORM (Write Once Read Many) disc, **23**
Wozniak, Steve, **51**
WP (Word Processing), **26**, 45, 55
wrapping, text, **34**
wrist rest, **47**
Write Once Read Many (WORM) disc, **23**
write to, **23**
WWW (World Wide Web), **30**, 55
WYSIWYG (What You See Is What You
        Get), **26**, 31, 55

Y

yellow (in printing), **10**

Z

Zero Insertion Force (ZIF) socket, **12**
ZIF (Zero Insertion Force) socket, **12**
zip disk, **23**, 41
zip drive, **23**
zooming, **34**
Zuse, Konrad, **51**
ZX81, **12**
ZX Spectrum, **12**

---

*Page numbers in bold type (eg **37**) show where to find the main explanation of a word or phrase.*

Every effort has been made to trace the copyright holders of the material in this book. If any rights have been omitted, the publishers offer their sincere apologies and will rectify this in any subsequent editions, following notification.

Usborne Publishing Ltd. has taken every care to ensure that the instructions in this book are accurate and suitable for their intended purpose. However, they are not responsible for the content of, and do not sponsor, any Web site not owned by them, including those listed below, nor are they responsible for any exposure to offensive or inaccurate material which may appear on the Web.

Apple, the Apple logo, Mac, Macintosh and QuickTime are trademarks of Apple Computer, Inc., registered in the United States and other countries. Microsoft, the Microsoft logo, Microsoft Internet Explorer, Microsoft Outlook, Microsoft Windows, Microsoft Windows 95, Microsoft Windows 98, Microsoft Windows CE and Microsoft Windows NT are either registered trademarks or trademarks of Microsoft Corporation in the US and other countries. Intel Inside, MMX, Pentium, Pentium II and Pentium Pro are either registered trademarks or trademarks of Intel Corporation in the US and other countries. RealPlayer is either a registered trademark or trademark of RealNetworks, Inc. in the United States and other countries. Shockwave is a trademark of Macromedia, Inc.

The publishers are grateful to the following organizations and individuals for permission to reproduce material:

Cover: (Hewlett-Packard Pavilion Multimedia PC, also p1) Courtesy of Hewlett-Packard; (CAD wire frame and rendered jet) Images produced in Autosketch for Autodesk, © Autodesk Ltd.
p2: (Combat game - "Cyclones", Space game - "Commander Blood") Mindscape International Ltd; (MIDI recording software) Cubase software by Steinberg; (Computer-generated map) ERDAS (UK) Ltd; (Paint package graphics of skittles) Softimage; (Ambient music graphics) Visuals from the Future Sound of London album "Lifeforms" courtesy of Virgin Records; (Computer-Aided Design image of car) Volkswagen.
p3: (Microsoft® Natural® keyboard, also p47) Photo used with permission from Microsoft Corporation; (CD-ROM drive) Aztech UK Ltd; (Optical disc) Philips; (Dongle) Software Security; (Inkjet printer) Used by permission of Hewlett-Packard; (Digital video camera, also p17) © 1998 Connectix Corporation; (Pace Modem, also on p19) PMC Consumer Electronics Ltd, manufacturer of peripherals for the PC; (Tamagotchi, also p42) Tamagotchi ™ and © 1996-1997 Bandai Co., Ltd.; (Clip-on trackball) Watford Electronics Ltd; (Graphics tablet) c-star Software.
p6: (Microsoft Windows logo, also p26) © Microsoft Ltd.
p10: (Colour inkjet printer, photo-quality printer) Used by permission of Hewlett-Packard; (Laser printer) Courtesy of Epson Ltd.
p12: (Apple Mac computer, Apple Computer logo, also p6) Apple Computer UK Ltd.
p13: (Personal organizer HP 300 LX, palmtop 620LX Infrared) Used by permission of Hewlett-Packard.
p14: (Charles Babbage) © Dr Jeremy Burgess/Science Photo Library.
p15: (Microwave oven) Whirlpool UK; (Dedicated Word Processor) Canon (UK) Ltd; (CAT scan of hand) © Robert Chase/Science Photo Library.
p16: (Long-distance mouse) Propoint remote pointing device available from LTS; (Graphics tablet) c-star Software.
p17: (Plotter) Used by permission of Hewlett-Packard.
p18: (Fibre-optic cable) © Adam Hart-Davis/Science Photo Library.
p19: (Desktop modem, Modem card) U.S. Robotics, Ltd.
p21: (Close-up of chip's surface) © David Scharf/Science Photo Library.
p24: (Icons) © Microsoft Ltd.
p25: (Games software) Europress Software Ltd; (Graphics software) Reproduced using RenderWare® courtesy of Criterion Software Ltd; (Computer-Aided Design software) Image produced in Autosketch for Autodesk, © Autodesk Ltd.
p27: (Business software users) © Tim Brown/Tony Stone Worldwide Photolibrary.
p28: (Computer network connections on the NSFNET) © NCSA, University of Illinois/Science Photo Library.
p29: (E-mail window) Copyright 1998 Netscape Communications Corp. Used with permission. All rights reserved. This electronic file or page may not be reprinted or copied without the express written permission of Netscape. Netscape Communications Corporation has not authorized, sponsored, or endorsed, or approved this publication and is not responsible for its content. Netscape and the Netscape Communications Corporate Logos, are trademarks and trade names of Netscape Communications Corporation. All other product names and/or logos are trademarks of their respective owners; (Marsupial frog) © Dr Morley Read/Science Photo Library.
p30: (White House) With thanks to the White House; (barnesandnoble.com, also on p33) Site used with permission. http://www.barnesandnoble.com/; (NASA) With thanks to NASA; (Microsoft Internet Explorer) Screen shot reprinted by permission from Microsoft Corporation.
p31: (Yahoo!) Yahoo! text and artwork copyright © 1998 by Yahoo! Inc. all rights reserved. Yahoo! and the Yahoo! logo are trademarks of Yahoo! Inc.; (AltaVista) Reproduced with the permission of AltaVista. AltaVista and the AltaVista logo are trademarks of AltaVista; (Microsoft Front Page Express) Screen shot reprinted by permission from Microsoft Corporation; (Java) Courtesy of H.K. Gutka.
p32: (Avatars/chat room) Courtesy of Electronic Communities; (Virtual Pool 2) Interplay Productions Limited; (Monopoly) Courtesy of Hasbro Interactive; (Ultimate Race Pro) © 1996/1998 Kalisto Technologies. All rights reserved. Ultimate Race Pro and Kalisto Technologies are trademarks of Kalisto Technologies. Microprose is a registered trademark of Microprose Ltd.
p33: (RSACi) Copyright RSACi, used with permission; (Net Nanny) Site used with permission, http://www.netnanny.com; (SurfWatch) SurfWatch, the pioneer of, and leader in, Internet filtering software.
p34: (Computer-generated map) ERDAS (UK) Ltd.
p35: (CAD wire frame and rendered jet, CAD engine parts, CAD building) Images produced in Autosketch for Autodesk, © Autodesk Ltd; (Virtual Reality garage) Virtual Reality product range, Superscape (Virtual Reality software).
p36: (Mouse) Marc Carey.
p37: (Paint package graphics of hangar and skittles) SOFTIMAGE; (Paint effects software - transparencies showing graphics) Flame Editing Interface, Discreet Logic (UK) Ltd.; (Fractal art) © Dr Fred Espenak/Science Photo Library; (3-D model) © Mike Agliolo/Science Photo Library.
p39: (Inbetweening graphics) Copyright © Cambridge Animation Systems; (Animated monster) SOFTIMAGE.
p40: (MIDI recording software) Cubase software by STEINBERG; (Scientist analyzing word patterns) © Hank Morgan/Science Photo Library; (Woman using DragonDictate voice recognition software) Dragon Systems UK Ltd.
p41: (Electronic keyboard) Yamaha-Kemble Music (UK) Ltd; (Electronic drum kit) Roland UK Ltd; (Ambient music graphics) Visuals from the Future Sound of London album "Lifeforms" courtesy of Virgin Records; (MiniDisc player) Sony.
p42: (Combat game - "Cyclones", Space game - "Commander Blood") Mindscape International Ltd; (Racing game - "The Need for Speed") Electronic Arts; (Virtual reality user wearing VR gear) © James King-Holmes/W Industries/Science Photo Library.
p43: (Multimedia PC) Western Systems; (Concept 90 Flight Simulator) Thomson Training & Simulation.
p46: (Earthed mouse mat) DAHLE (Anti-static Mat); (Disk drive lock) IDS; (Dongle) Software Security; (Screen saver) Screen shot reprinted by permission from Microsoft Corporation.
p47: (Disk Doctor graphic) Reproduced with the permission of SYMANTEC and Sentrybox. Usborne Publishing Ltd will respect all Symantec Corporation's copyrights. (Hand affected by carpal tunnel syndrome) © Custom Medical Stock Photo/Science Photo Library; (Mouse mat with built-in wrist rest) Acco-Rexel; (Hand-shaped mouse) Gem Distribution.
p48: (Animatronic robotic dinosaur) The Natural History Museum, London; (Child using computer) © David Young Wolff/Tony Stone Images.
p49: (Woman telecommuting) © David Hanover/Tony Stone Images; (Smart card used as reference) With thanks to London Transport Buses BEST project; (Hand-held computer terminal) Remanco Systems Limited.
p50: (Photo of Andrew Walker using functional electronic stimulus system) Reproduced by kind permission of Andrew Walker and ASPIRE (Association for Spinal Injury, Research, Rehabilitation and Reintegration), with thanks to Fiona Barr; (Sony PlayStation, Widescreen television) Sony.
p51: (Ada Lovelace) Mary Evans Picture Library; (William Gibson) Penguin Books Ltd.
p52: ("Manny" Android) © US Department of Energy/Science Photo Library; (Virtual Reality brain imaging) © Peter Menzel/Science Photo Library.
p53: (Wearable) © Sam Ogden/Science Photo Library.

The publishers would like to thank Apple Computer Ltd, IBM UK Ltd, Intel Corporation UK Ltd, Microsoft UK Ltd, and Dan Jones (composer) for their help.